New Industrial Spaces

Studies in Society and Space

Series editors **A J Scott** and **M Storper**

1 **Capital, the state, and regional development** M F Dunford
2 **Wrecking a region** R Hudson
3 **New industrial spaces** A J Scott

P
Pion Limited, 207 Brondesbury Park, London NW2 5JN

New Industrial Spaces

Flexible Production Organization
and Regional Development
in North America
and Western Europe

A J Scott

P Pion Limited, 207 Brondesbury Park, London NW2 5JN

ISBN 0 85086 131 4

Printed in Great Britain by Page Bros (Norwich) Limited

This book is intended as a companion volume to my recently published *Metropolis: From the Division of Labor to Urban Form* (University of California Press, Berkeley and Los Angeles, 1988). Where that book dealt with problems of urbanization, the present volume is focused above all on recent changes in processes and patterns of regional development. Both books, however, are based on similar theoretical premises, and a common structure of argument runs through both. Their point of departure resides in the idea that the locational structure of the space-economy of capitalism can usefully be analyzed in terms of the dynamics of the social division of labor. These dynamics create, as I shall attempt to demonstrate, powerful tendencies to geographical convergence and agglomeration in the production system, and hence to the formation of concentrated points of economic growth at selected locations. The same dynamics constitute a central analytical moment in any attempt to understand the logic of spatial development in the current conjuncture, marked as it is by a strong turn from Fordist to flexible forms of production organization. I show that this turn is also associated with a series of complex local labor-market transformations that independently heighten tendencies to locational agglomeration. All of these phenomena are, in addition, imbricated within a variety of sociopolitical arrangements that modulate the detailed ways in which they are concretely expressed on the landscape of capitalism. In the present volume, I provide a brief interpretation of these arrangements by reference to contemporary notions about regimes of accumulation and modes of social regulation. It is my hope that both books, taken together, will help to elucidate many of the important and deeply rooted changes that are currently working their effects on urban and regional systems throughout the advanced capitalist nations.

This book could not have been written without the generous support that I have been privileged to receive over the last few years. First of all I wish to thank the John Simon Guggenheim Memorial Foundation for awarding me a fellowship in 1986–1987 that allowed me to take time off from my teaching obligations at the University of California–Los Angeles to write the book. The National Science Foundation funded two major research projects (under grant numbers SES 8204376 and SES 8414398) from 1982 to 1987, and with this support I was able to accomplish the detailed and costly empirical investigations that lie in the background of all the arguments deployed below. The Institute of Industrial Relations and the College Institute of the College of Letters and Science, both at the University of California–Los Angeles, generously provided supplemental research funding. Last, I express my gratitude to the Centre de Recherche sur l'Industrie et l'Aménagement at the Institut de Géographie, University of Paris I, for its hospitality over the year 1986–87.

Chapter 7 is based on a paper that I wrote jointly with David Angel, and which was published in *Environment and Planning A* (volume 19, pages 875–912). I wish to acknowledge David Angel's contribution to this paper, and to thank him for his generous permission to incorporate parts of it into the present book. I also thank Pion Ltd, the copyright holders, for allowing me to reprint this material here. Andrew Sayer and Michael Storper provided useful comments on an early draft of this book, and these comments have helped me in subsequent revisions. As is usual in these matters, my critics are fully exonerated from any responsibility for what is said, and not said, in the pages that follow.

A J Scott

Contents

1

Introduction

From the perspective of an observer situated in, say, the mid-1950s, the geographical outlines of the world's major capitalist economies must have looked reassuringly stable and predictable. Each of these economies seemed roughly and broadly to be split into two major spatial realms, namely, on the one hand, a core of large manufacturing regions containing dense concentrations of population and economic activity, and on the other hand, peripheral expanses of comparatively less well-developed territory much given to agriculture and local service activities, and with occasional small clusters of industrial employment in a few favored places. The two realms were functionally interrelated with one another via accelerating shifts of routinized production units from the core to the periphery, and the migration of labor (especially skilled labor) in the opposite direction. At the same time, the contrasts between the core and the periphery appeared to many theorists to be extremely durable, and, if anything, to be intensifying (Hirschman, 1958; Myrdal, 1957). At best, perhaps, spatial adjustment processes might bring about factor-price equalization (cf Borts and Stein, 1964), but scarcely equality in levels of industrial and urban development. With the exception of patently overoptimistic assessments by neoclassical regional economists, most analysts of the situation in the postwar decades came to one version or another of the conclusion that leading regions tend endemically to lead and lagging regions to lag, and that the disparities between them thus continually widen.

The leading regions of North America and Western Europe had, indeed, a number of significant in-built developmental advantages. Over much of the present century, the economies of the great manufacturing regions, such as the Northeast of the United States, the Midlands of England, or the Rhine–Ruhr area of Germany, had evolved into powerful engines of production based on expanding propulsive sectors. These sectors consisted in varying degree of heavy industry (coal, steel, and chemicals for the most part) along with metallurgical and assembly industries engaged in the fabrication of outputs such as machinery, cars, household appliances, and so on. The latter sectors were organized preeminently in conformity with Fordist principles of labor management and work involving process-flow and assembly-line methods of production and much technical division of labor. Overall economic prosperity and social stability were secured after the 1930s as Keynesian macroeconomic policy was steadily elaborated and as the welfare state emerged into a full-blown program of social security. On these foundations, the major capitalist economies expanded rapidly and irresistibly, as manifest above all in the long postwar boom stretching from the 1950s to the late 1960s and early 1970s.

These events were not, of course, free from problems and tensions. A number of older industrial areas, such as the Appalachian region and

New England in the USA, or Clydeside and Lancashire in Britain showed definite signs of stress even during the postwar boom years. Over the same period, throughout North America and Western Europe, manufacturing plants steadily abandoned the central parts of large metropolitan regions in favor of locations in the suburbs and even further afield. Concomitantly, by the late 1950s and early 1960s, the beginnings of a disquieting shift offshore of certain industrial sectors (such as textiles and shoes) were already perceptible. Despite these recurrent symptoms of the fluidity of capitalist structures of production and work, there was little or no apprehension in any of the research being carried out on regional development in the 1950s and 1960s that the industrial geography of the advanced capitalist societies was about to be turned on its head. Instead, debate tended to focus on whether or not and to what degree regional disparities could be reduced, while taking the existing geographical pattern of industrialization and urbanization as a relatively fixed point of reference.

Over the 1970s, however, this pattern began to shift dramatically. As the long postwar boom came to an end, the major capitalist economies of North America and Western Europe entered into a long period of crisis and readjustment which, even now, has still not fully run its course. More and more of the traditional basic industries of the core regions—industries such as steel, shipbuilding, car assembly, machinery, electrical goods, and so on— were now moving at an alarming rate out to the world periphery in order to take advantage of its increasingly attractive production conditions (most notably its low wages and regressive labor relations). One effect of these movements was the formation of a so-called new international division of labor (cf Fröbel et al, 1980). Simultaneously, intensified competition from Japan and the newly industrializing countries was having strongly negative effects on whole production sectors in North America and Western Europe. Runaway inflation, combined with persistently high rates of unemployment and falling industrial productivity, added to the difficulties of the major capitalist economies, as did the severe oil shocks of the 1970s.

The net result of these developments was a major crisis of the core industrial regions of North America and Western Europe. The crisis became first apparent in the late 1960s in Britain and the United States, and it spread over the early 1970s to France, Italy, and West Germany. In many formerly prosperous industrial regions, investment in new plant and machinery now slowed to a trickle, and large units of fixed capital were written off in an epidemic of factory closures and employment cutbacks. In some places, unemployment reached levels not seen since the 1930s. As a result, many working-class communities were devastated, and the political strength of labor unions was severely depleted. In the United States, several major cities were brought to the very brink of bankruptcy as their tax bases shrank in response to their declining economies.

In the face of these deepening predicaments, a new literature of industrial crisis began to make its appearance towards the end of the 1970s, as represented most notably by Bluestone and Harrison (1982) in the United States, Massey and Meegan (1982) in Britain, and Stoffaës (1978) in France, all of whom struggled in different ways to articulate an explicitly political response to the problem. This literature is in general marked by deeply pessimistic diagnoses of the situation in the old industrial regions and sectors, as revealed by a vocabulary in which such terms as job loss, redundancy, unemployment, deindustrialization, restructuring, decentralization, and so on abound. The dynamic industrial system based on Fordist forms of production organization which had been steadily put into place since the opening decades of the century seemed now, in its very homelands, to be on the point of collapse. In the United States, the Carter presidency represented, in political terms, the last gasp of the old tripartite social order built up around oligopolistic growth poles, Keynesian macroeconomic policy, and the social safety net of the welfare state. As this order began to crumble, so too did much of its industrial base in the old Manufacturing Belt.

As it happens, and even as these processes of decay and decline were reaching their greatest peak of intensity, some regions in some of the advanced capitalist nations were developing counter to the general trend, and were actually experiencing rapid rates of formation of new manufacturing capital and rapid rates of employment growth (see figure 1.1). These were regions located for the most part in a series of marginal areas which over the 1950s and 1960s had been greatly overshadowed by the main centers of industrial production. In many cases, too, they were regions without any established tradition of industrialization and whose development began virtually ab initio some time during or after the 1950s. Often, the very existence of these regions was overlooked in the great debates on

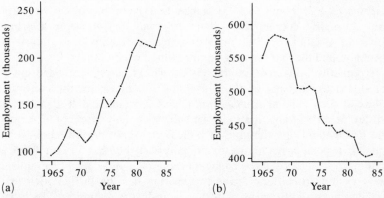

Figure 1.1. Contrasting patterns of manufacturing employment in two SMSAs, 1965–84: (a) Orange County, CA, and (b) Philadelphia, PA. Source of data: *County Business Patterns* and *Employment Hours and Earnings, States and Areas*, Bulletin 1370-17 and Bulletin 1370-19.

regional development in the 1960s and 1970s; or, if their existence was remarked upon, they were for the most part simply seen as passive recipients of decentralized units of capital originating in core regions. Insofar as it goes, this connection to decentralization processes is not necessarily a bad point of departure for analysis, though it also needs to be complemented (as we shall see) by additional insights about processes of industrial organization and regional development, and these were rarely forthcoming to begin with.

Even so, an alternative perspective on these processes began slowly to emerge over the 1970s and 1980s. One of the first of the new growth regions of the recent past to receive analytical attention was the zone of high-technology industrial development that had sprung up along Route 128 in the western outskirts of Boston (Roberts and Wainer, 1968), though the wider significance of this phenomenon as a harbinger of future patterns of economic and spatial transformation was not at first fully appreciated. In 1977 Bagnasco published his *Tre Italie* which dealt with an emerging model of industrialization in northeastern and central Italy based on traditional crafts and fragmented units of production; the book, however, was thoroughly ignored by English-language scholars at the time of its publication, and even in Italy its portentous message was perhaps not initially clearly understood. By the early 1980s, the Silicon Valley phenomenon was beginning to provoke a modest stream of literature on the theme of ascending growth regions, as exemplified by the writings of Saxenian (1983) or Rogers and Larson (1984). Then, by the mid-1980s, a flood of studies on the geography of high-technology industry started to appear, showing decisively that many different parts of North America and Western Europe had not only weathered the storm of restructuring in the 1970s, but were now also functioning as major foci of industrial innovation and expansion in their own right. It was now quite evident, in brief, that a series of *new industrial spaces* had come into existence and were beginning to form important alternative centers of capitalist accumulation based on a strong social division of labor, proliferations of small to medium-sized industrial establishments, and the marked reagglomeration of production.

Our hypothetical observer in the 1950s would surely not have given much credence to portents of these eventual outcomes; on the contrary, projections of then current trends would have led (and did lead) to altogether different sorts of anticipations. And yet, with the wisdom of historical hindsight it is evident that the kind of radical turnabout described above is by no means a peculiarity of the immediate past, but has in fact been a persistent episodic feature of the changing economic landscape of capitalism over the very long run. Behind this proposition lies the further idea that there are innumerable different pathways to industrialization and regional development in capitalism, and that the recently hegemonic model of Fordist mass production, large growth poles, and dense regional concentrations of overgrown manufacturing cities is far from representing the inevitable historical and geographical destiny of modern industrial society. To the contrary, other very different sorts of models are currently an open possibility for many of the advanced capitalist economies (cf Piore and Sabel, 1984). How, we might ask, can we begin to approach the extended field of enquiry suggested by these remarks? How and why do ruptures in previously established spatiotemporal pathways to industrialization occur? Why precisely did the core manufacturing regions of North America and Western Europe fall into crisis after the late 1960s, and what factors lie behind the rise of the new industrial spaces alluded to above? How will these spaces develop in the future? Will they, in their turn, eventually enter into a period of economic stagnation and decline? Can we construct a theoretical language for dealing with issues like these? If so, what lessons can this language teach us about problems of human geography in general?

This book is intended as a preliminary attempt to address some of these questions by means of both theoretical analysis and empirical description. I start off with a discussion of some of the macrosocial forces that seem to me to help account for periodic shifts in the structure of the space-economy of capitalism. I then focus intently on a set of mesolevel processes that are, I claim, of particular relevance to any effort to understand the detailed logic of the important locational changes currently going on in North America and Western Europe. These processes concern above all the institutional form of the firm, the organization of production systems, and the division of labor. From this vantage point, I seek to show how strong agglomeration effects come into existence in certain places and thus give rise to localized territorial complexes of economic production and human activity. I also show how these effects intersect with a series of contingent social phenomena in such a way as to secure (or destroy) sociospatial reproduction of the same complexes. In an attempt to exemplify and expand upon these theoretical analyses I then develop three detailed empirical case studies that provide a many-sided and cross-cultural fix on their central meaning. The case studies concern, first, the Third Italy with its burgeoning artisanal forms of industrial production; second, the Scientific City of the southern Paris region, which represents a new high-technology industrial growth center of major proportions; and, third, Silicon Valley, whose dynamics I attempt to capture by means of a statistical comparison between semiconductor producers located in the Valley and producers at other locations in the United States. In the final chapter of the book, I offer a synthesis of all the main arguments, but emphasize the importance of a cultural/political (as well as a purely economic) comprehension of industrialization processes.

Throughout the book, I pay particular attention to very recent changes in the geography of manufacturing. From what I have already said, however, it is evident that I believe the book has much wider analytical significance than this. In particular, it represents a definite attempt to reformulate certain key propositions in the theories of location and regional development, and in this sense alone it has relevance to the investigation of a yet more comprehensive set of phenomena than those dealt with in the case-study material laid out below. I should add that certain extensions of the argument developed in the book lead on logically to questions of the multinational enterprise and the international division of labor. For the most part, I refrain from broaching these questions directly, though they must be seen as important background elements to all that follows.

Accumulation and the space-economy

One of the great themes of political economy is the restless, fluid character of capitalism. Under the pressures of accumulation the social world is continually being transformed and retransformed. Schumpeter (1950) evoked the same theme with his celebrated description of capitalist dynamics as an endless surge of creative destruction. As a consequence of this endemic fluidity, the dimensions of historical time and *geographical space* in capitalism are both marked by persistent change in the dual form of (a) marginal adjustments relative to a given basic pattern of development, and (b) occasional episodic ruptures or shifts as the sociospatial order of capitalism moves rapidly from one dominant configuration to another. The latter phenomenon is of especial interest here, for much of what follows is an attempt to decipher the major geographical consequences of the rise of a new industrial order in North America and Western Europe. We can begin to approach an understanding of the general significance of this pheno-menon through a review of some ideas about the technological and institutional foundations of capitalist production systems.

Technological–institutional structures of production and accumulation

At the core of the capitalist economy lies the process of commodity production with its overarching logic of profit-seeking economic activity and accumulation of capital. This process is an endemic feature of capital-ism and yet it is also susceptible to considerable variation in the concrete technological and institutional shapes it assumes at different historical moments. To exemplify the point, we need only reflect on the many con-trasts between such historical episodes as the putting-out phase of early capitalism, the classical period of 19th century capitalist development focused on factory forms of work organization, or the era of Fordist mass production that stretched from the early decades of the present century down to the 1960s and 1970s. Such episodes constitute more or less distinctive technological–institutional structures of production and accumulation, though the breaks between them are rarely, if ever, clearly articulated, and a dominant structural form may well exist side by side with a series of alternative ways of organizing production. Hence, small-scale artisanal production continued to flourish widely throughout the era of Fordist industrialization; and, if today a new sort of production system seems to be on the point of breaking forth in the advanced capitalist societies, Fordist production relations are very far from disappearing altogether.

The notion of a technological–institutional structure of production and accumulation is not unlike the dual concept of a regime of accumulation (a given set of capitalist production relations) and a cognate mode of social regulation (a series of sociopolitical arrangements enabling the regime to operate over time) proposed in recent years by theorists of the French Regulationist School (cf Aglietta, 1979; Boyer, 1986; Lipietz, 1986). I shall attempt here to provide some further insights into the technological and institutional logic of capitalism on the basis of arguments put forward by these theorists. These arguments provide conceptual tools for identifying distinctive moments of capitalist economic development. Analogous sets of tools have been proposed in terms of long waves (for example, by Mandel, 1980), or the temporal swarming of industrial innovations (Freeman et al, 1982), or the materialization of given technological paradigms (Dosi, 1984). Each of these ways of looking at the problem, like the regulationist approach, puts much emphasis on a view of economic history as a series of relatively long-run periods normalized around a given set of production relations embodied in an ensemble of critical sectors, and separated from one another by definite ruptures. The regulationist approach, however, has the merit of attempting to go beyond temporal or technological abstractions and of seeking to implicate the whole structure of social and economic relations in the analysis of the changing historical forms of industrial capitalism.

A regime of accumulation can be rather simply defined as a historically specific production apparatus (in capitalism) through which the surplus is generated, appropriated, and redeployed. The definition can be further refined by decomposing the notion of a regime into an articulation of four distinctive elements:
(a) a set of production techniques,
(b) a characteristic way of organizing production and labor relations,
(c) a distributional mechanism governing the appropriation and redeployment of the surplus,
(d) a process of aggregate demand driving forward the evolution of productive capacity.
These articulated elements of the production system then demarcate a regime of accumulation as a concretized form of the basic economic structures of commodity production (cf Boyer, 1986).

A regime of accumulation is thus a realization of a generalized capitalist production model [à la Sraffa (1960), say], but in such a way as to root its abstracted map of technical and social relations in tangible moments of economic history. These historically rooted relations determine the magnitude and rhythms of accumulation at any given time. However, they are also, in general, unable to function effectively purely on the basis of their own logic. They are continually susceptible to invasion by distortions and disequilibria that threaten their workability and impede their further development. Thus, smooth accumulation is forever being interrupted by dysfunctionalities such as recession, class conflicts, the formation of monopolies, trade imbalances, and the like. The ability of any regime of accumulation to survive is therefore dependent on the emergence of further sets of social relations that preserve it, for a time at least, from catastrophic internal collisions and breakdowns. These relations constitute a mode of social regulation. They are made up of a series of formal and informal structures of governance and stabilization ranging from the state, through business and labor associations, to modes of socialization which create ingrained habits of behavior, and so on. Some of these structures come into existence spontaneously; others are consciously designed and put into place in the effort to keep the production system on a reasonably even keel. No matter how they may originate, we need to guard against the blunt functionalist proposition that the regime of accumulation causes the mode of social regulation because that is what it needs in order to survive. That said, we may certainly allow ourselves the converse notion that realized regimes of accumulation survive in practice because, over their lifetimes, various regulatory mechanisms come into being. Presumably, in addition, the particular mode of social regulation that is in practice associated with a given regime of accumulation represents only one out of many alternative possibilities: each regime, in short, may potentially be regulated in a multiplicity of different ways. A crisis leading to a rupture in the regime of accumulation is then an episode in which the viability of the whole system is compromised, leading to a search for other ways of organizing production and other regulatory contexts.

These remarks may be exemplified concretely by the case of the regime of Fordist accumulation. The mass-production forms of industry characteristic of this type of accumulation are marked by a search for massive internal economies of scale based on process-flow and assembly-line methods, technical divisions of labor, and standardization of outputs. The Fordist elements of the system comprise, in their essentials, the deskilling of labor, by means of the fragmentation of work tasks combined with the integration of the human operator into the whole machinery of production in such a way as to reduce to the minimum, discretionary control over motions and rhythms of work. With steadily expanding demands for the outputs of mass-production industry, a rising horizon of corporate profits can generally be secured, and in the heyday of Fordist industry organized labor was accorded a share in this prosperity via wage increases and fringe benefits tied to productivity gains. As this system of production was put into place in the early decades of this century, it also came to be associated with a distinctive set of regulatory structures. Especially after the massive crisis of the system as represented by the great depression of 1929, central government manipulation of macroeconomic variables via Keynesian intervention, and social control by means of welfare legislation, became increasingly common. Thus, in society at large a widening social safety net helped to maintain a broad, if uneasy, social and industrial peace, just as it also helped to sustain the production–consumption nexus on which so much of the system depended for its continued expansion. Geographically, the system was represented by a series of growth pole industries concentrated in and around large industrial conurbations like Detroit, Birmingham,

Bochum – Dortmund, Turin, or the northern and northwestern suburbs of Paris. These conurbations housed a large and relatively affluent working class, and, particularly after the Second World War, they were the object of persistent urban planning interventions in an attempt to enhance their role as foci of social reproduction.

For a considerable time the regime of Fordist accumulation functioned remarkably well, until eventually undermined by its own success and the pressures of foreign competition. By the late 1960s and early 1970s severe and apparently intractable problems were starting to become evident. As we have seen, North American and European production systems were both by now internationalizing at a rapid rate, leaving behind widening pockets of unemployment in formerly thriving communities. Simultaneously, the saturation of domestic mass markets was beginning to impose severe limits on economic expansion. The oil shocks of the 1970s and the competitive incursions of imports from Japan and the newly industrializing countries on domestic markets only served to make these problems more acute. Simultaneously, Keynesian welfare-statist policy was becoming increasingly mired down in a deepening crisis of stagflation. The old established industrial regions of the advanced capitalist nations were, almost without exception, put under considerable stress by these events and many of them entered into a long downward spiral of job loss and unemployment that in most cases continues to the present day.

Out of this disarray, however, there started to emerge in the late 1970s and early 1980s, the outlines of a new dominant regime of accumulation and mode of social regulation, along with some important new forms of regional development in both North America and Western Europe. This new regime is focused above all on *flexibility* of production processes and labor markets and (in contradistinction to Fordist mass production) on the search for *external* economies of scale in the organization of the industrial apparatus. The roots of this regime can be traced back to the immediate postwar years, but the turning point seems above all to be represented by the rise of Reaganism in the United States and Thatcherism in Britain, and the later rightwards shift politically in other Western European democracies. These developments helped to rekindle the forces of economic competition, to encourage a new spirit of self-reliance and entrepreneurialism, and to reduce yet further the already depleted strength of the labor unions. The dominant features of this emerging system are even today not clearly distinguishable and there evidently remains a large margin of manoeuverability as to its eventual shape, though four main points can readily be made about its broad configuration. First, in all of the major capitalist economies (including Japan) experiments are now proceeding on a major scale with programmable and hence flexible forms of production automation. Second, flexibility is to an increasing degree also being secured by means of socially fragmented but interconnected and organizationally pliable units of economic activity. Third, rigidities in the employment relation are rapidly decomposing on a wide front and more fluid internal and external labor-market structures are making their appearance as a consequence. Fourth, the old regulatory practices involving the Keynesian welfare-statism of the recent past are in varying degrees being actively dismantled and a new emphasis placed on economic and social privatization combined (in the USA) with unprecedentedly high federal expenditures on armaments and defense. These expenditures function as one of the central motors of growth of the contemporary US economy and they now sustain a whole series of high-technology industrial sectors and regions.

At the same time, the emerging regime of flexible accumulation is physically founded on a series of new ensembles (or collections) of production sectors. Two such ensembles are of particular relevance to the question of new industrial spaces in contemporary capitalism, and they may be enumerated immediately as (a) revivified craft and design-intensive industries producing outputs (such as clothing, furniture, jewelry, shoes, textiles, and so on) largely but not exclusively for final consumption, and (b) various kinds of high-technology industries and their associated phalanxes of input suppliers and dependent subcontractors. There is, in addition, a third significant new flexible ensemble consisting of a rapidly expanding set of sectors providing an immense variety of business, financial, and personal services essential to the efficient economic and social functioning of contemporary capitalism. In this book, I shall be dealing primarily with the first two of these three ensembles, though I shall make frequent reference to the service ensemble where this is appropriate to the argument. Even older mass-production forms of industry have not been immune from the winds of change currently sweeping the major capitalist economies, and many are shedding their erstwhile hidebound modes of operation in favor of more flexible technological-*cum*-organizational structures imbricated in just-in-time linkage partnerships and with reconstructed systems of labor relations based on neo-Fordist principles.

In addition to the recent social and political changes that have helped to usher in these various transformations of the production systems of North America and Western Europe, the rise of the modern electronics industry has also been a critical (technical) factor. This industry is both a centrally symptomatic sector of the new regime and a general precondition of augmented production flexibility in the economy at large. Electronics is critical to the new regime, for it provides the means of performing work (calculating, communicating, controlling, data processing, and measuring) without the intermediation of mechanical devices.

The problem of geographic change
Just as capitalist society in its totality evolves through a combination of small-scale marginal changes superimposed on less frequent but more dramatic episodic shifts, so also does the locational structure of production, and with it the geographical coordinates of social life in general. At any

particular instant, a dominant, stable pattern of production locations will usually be observable, and, relative to this pattern, various minor adjustments will in all likelihood be in course. However, with a major break involving a shift from one regime of accumulation to another, the range and diversity of possible locational outcomes are greatly extended. This is all the more the case where the shift is accompanied by much technological innovation and the rise of novel production ensembles. As this shift occurs, a continuum of potential spatial responses will usually also be observable, ranging from the selective *internal* recolonization of industrial regions formed in earlier regimes of accumulation to the *external* reconstruction of industrial activity in new geographical areas, with any number of possible intermediate outcomes between these two extremes (cf Scott and Storper, 1987). Although this book is focused preeminently on clear-cut cases of the external response to the ongoing shift from Fordism to flexible accumulation, I shall nonetheless make some brief observations in these introductory remarks about the entire range of current spatial responses to the shift. I begin with a recapitulation of some of the reasons why geographical environments shaped under the direct experience of Fordism are increasingly hostile to new industrial investments generally and above all to the formation of flexible production complexes.

In the old industrial regions of North America and Western Europe an assemblage of major urban–industrial agglomerations had become fully formed by the early decades of the 20th century. These agglomerations constituted a network of interconnected growth centers. With the progressive installation and intensification of the regime of Fordist accumulation, strong propulsive impulses and economic multiplier effects began to flow backwards and forwards through this network of growth centers. The same centers were (as they are still today) populated by a labor force rooted through housing and community structures to the local area. Over a number of generations, the labor force in each center tended to acquire forms of consciousness and culture combining elements of both a generalized class character and experience of the particular workaday world of the given center. Rates of worker unionization were high, especially in large plants where the tasks of political organizing were relatively easy to accomplish. Right down to the 1960s and early 1970s, workers continued, through their union representatives, to amass significant rights and entitlements in the workplace and to keep wages rising upwards, all of which tended to hem in managerial strategies, to restrict productivity, and to reduce competitiveness. Producers' costs were also steadily inflated by rising land prices, high local tax rates, negative externalities (such as congestion and pollution), and the like. In spite of these problems, producers had no option over much of the period of active growth of Fordist industry but to continue to locate in those centers, for they possessed precisely the kinds of agglomeration economies (that is, ready access to appropriate suppliers, subcontractors, and markets; and a labor force embodying a full range of requisite skills and habituated to the norms and rhythms of mass production) that were essential for the profitable deployment of capital. Only those kinds of plants that had successfully eliminated the need for such agglomeration economies (for example, by massive routinization and deskilling of production processes) were able to decentralize away from this zone of rising predicaments. By the 1970s, foreign competition was helping to make those predicaments acute indeed, thus provoking technological change in the direction of increased routinization and deskilling and leading to accelerated decentralization of capital.

Meanwhile, as the seeds of the regime of flexible accumulation were germinating in the 1960s and 1970s, a further set of locational transformations was in the making. These consist of the twofold tendency to (a) a definite spatial *reagglomeration* of production in selected areas, combined with (b) active evasion of labor pools dominated now or in the recent past by Fordist industry. The net result is that significant numbers of new growth centers based on flexible production systems have started to spring up in a series of geographical spaces that are either socially insulated or (more importantly for present purposes) geographically insulated from the main foci of earlier rounds of Fordist industrialization. In either case the net result is that flexible production sectors have been able to cut corners around the traditional working class, with its organizational bases in large labor unions and its accumulated historical experience of the capital – labor relation. These remarks may be further deepened by reference to our three major production ensembles mentioned earlier.

In the first place, flexible design-intensive craft industries are at the present time growing rapidly both in inner-city areas in certain large metropolitan regions and in a variety of new (or resurgent) industrial spaces. The first case is represented by industries such as clothing, furniture, and jewelry in major cities like New York, Los Angeles, Paris, and so on. These industries usually comprise a large sweatshop component, and they have grown of late on the basis of major new waves of immigration (for example, Asians and Latinos in the United States, or North Africans, Portuguese, and Turks in France). The second case is represented by expanding craft industry centers in areas such as Denmark, southern Germany, the Jura region of Switzerland, parts of France, central Portugal, and elsewhere in Western Europe. A particularly dramatic example of this kind of industrial development is provided by the growth since the 1950s of the traditional towns of northeast and central Italy, with their production systems geared to the fabrication of high-quality consumer goods such as ceramics, furniture, shoes, sporting goods, and textiles. The Italian case is dealt with in considerably more detail in chapter 5.

In the second place, high-technology industry has grown apace at a wide variety of locations under the regime of flexible accumulation. These locations include a number of suburban sites next to major cities in older and newer industrial areas in both North America and Western Europe, such as Boston's Route 128, Orange County and Silicon Valley in California, the M4 Corridor in southern England, or the Scientific City of the southern Paris region. They also include various small to medium-sized towns in formerly peripheral areas such as Austin, Boulder, or Colorado Springs in the USA, and Cambridge, Grenoble, Montpellier, or Sophia Antipolis in Europe. In most of these cases, employment is based on segmented local labor markets comprising skilled managerial and technical cadres on the one side and disorganized malleable fractions of the labor force (such as women and immigrants) on the other side.

In the third place, office and business service activities, have expanded rapidly in the central business districts of major metropolitan regions as well as in selected suburban communities. These activities are based preferentially on white-collar labor (including large numbers of low-wage female workers). They are typically extremely diversified as a whole and much given to agglomerative locational behavior.

As already indicated, some of the older mass-production industries in North America and Western Europe have also recently been subject to similar transformations based on increased flexibilization of production arrangements. This has sometimes occurred in situ, as in the case of the Detroit car industry, and sometimes it has been associated with dramatic locational readjustments, as in the case of General Motors' proposed Saturn project at Spring Hill, Tennessee. Developments like these have almost always been combined with the renegotiation of union contracts in ways that have severely curtailed workers' expectations, and especially those of entry level workers (cf Clark, 1986).

Flexible production systems thus represent radically new kinds of organizational and labor-market structures with locational tendencies that contrast markedly to those of Fordist mass production. As we have seen above, flexible production systems are found in a wide diversity of different locations, though these are almost always some distance—socially or geographically—from the major foci of Fordist industrialization. In particular, many kinds of flexible production sectors (craft and high-technology sectors above all) have a certain predisposition to locate in new industrial spaces lying far beyond the geographical confines of the hitherto dominant core areas of economic activity and regional expansion. These spaces represent environments where, as the turn to flexible production organization has become consolidated as a major trend, industrial activities are being steadily recreated on alternative sociospatial foundations. This has involved major shifts in investment from locations adjacent to traditional working-class communities to alternative production sites with a very different cultural and political character. At such sites, the local history of capitalism is, as it were, being reconstructed anew. Thus, for example, in the US Sunbelt, clusters of high-technology industry have typically taken root in politically conservative areas without any significant prior industrial development.

Important social transformations of these areas have, of course, subsequently occurred, especially where the growth of jobs and population has been rapid. Even so, local firms have thus far been largely successful in resisting attempts to unionize the labor force. Municipal politics are often, in addition, dominated by growth coalitions with a strong pro-business orientation. The new industrial spaces of Western Europe also pose innumerable questions about the interrelations between industrialization and the local cultural/political climate. These Western European cases range from areas that are just as conservative as any Sunbelt community to areas with quite radical political traditions, above all in parts of northeast and central Italy. The complex problems raised by these relationships are discussed in chapters 5 and 6. In each particular case, in both North America and Western Europe, a definite way out of prior and increasingly problematical conditions of accumulation has been accomplished by these shifts from Fordism to flexibility and from old to new industrial spaces.

One further major point needs to be made about the mechanisms underlying the process of spatial switching. To understand this process a little more clearly, we need to recall that, as the ascending regime of flexible accumulation was in its earliest stages of development, new ensembles of production sectors started to move into positions of economic prominence. Let us consider here the admittedly special (but extraordinarily important) case of high-technology industry. This kind of industry had at the outset very different locational needs from those of the sectors that dominated the now waning Fordist regime of accumulation, and, in the early innovative phases, these needs were in any case extremely generalized and diffuse. More broadly, because the ascending regime brought with it new and unforeseen kinds of technologies, linkages, and labor demands, a *window of locational opportunity* opened widely, and, for a time at least, it was possible for producers to choose from an enormous array of locational alternatives. As it happens, in the case of high-technology industry in the United States, the balance was tipped in favor of the Sunbelt with its absence of strong union traditions and its favorable business climate. Even within this specific geographic realm, the choice of locational options was still vast. Those specific areas that did begin to develop advanced rapidly as the play of agglomeration and urbanization economies gave them an increasingly competitive edge over other areas. In this manner, the window of locational opportunity alluded to above has in part begun to close around places that made an early start. By the same token, the main Sunbelt growth centers whose origins date back to the 1950s and 1960s seem now to be in the process of developing as the established core regions of the new high-technology ensemble.

Through these processes of locational transformation, the regime of flexible accumulation is currently assuming distinctive geographical outlines focused on a number of particular regions where economic growth is proceeding with special intensity. No doubt the emergence of other regimes of accumulation at past times has also been accompanied both by internal and by external transformations of basic geographical patterns, though certainly with much idiosyncrasy in each case, as always in matters of historical eventuation. A major question at this stage is whether or not (despite this idiosyncrasy) it is possible to abstract in theoretical terms some of the central organizational and locational dynamics underlying these transformations. In what now follows, I propose to respond affirmatively to this question by means of an investigation into some relevant processes of firm formation, the social division of labor, and spatial change. These processes are of major significance for any attempt to comprehend the geography of the new regime of flexible accumulation, though they are also, of course, operative (with varying specific effects) in all previous rounds of capitalist industrialization. They ensure that once a region has begun to develop, even if by pure chance, its further expansion is then often sustained by a self-reinforcing logic of agglomeration and growth. The new industrial spaces of North America and Western Europe are strongly subject to this logic.

3

The organization of industrial production

Towards an analysis

I have shown how the broad outlines of economic geography at any given time are defined by reference to a prevailing regime of accumulation and how changes in the latter entail corresponding transformations of the former. In other words, the pattern of spatiality, like the structure of temporality, is fixed by the modalities and tempos of specific historical forms of accumulation. This is an important and useful idea that helps to illuminate various aspects of macrogeographic change, though it also still leaves much unsaid about detailed locational processes and outcomes. Without some complementary analytical apparatus, we are not likely to make much progress in attempts to comprehend how the finely textured scenarios of spatial development in any given regime of accumulation are played out in practice.

The new industrial spaces that have come into being in the new regime of flexible accumulation are typified, above all, by a resurgence of the phenomena of the social division of labor and agglomeration, combined with rapid rates of local growth. As shown earlier, these new industrial spaces tend to coincide with areas removed from previous rounds of Fordist economic development. Often enough these are areas that seem at the outset to have had few predispositions marking them out for incipient industrialization. Here I am going somewhat against the grain of a certain body of recent literature on the geography of high-technology industry which evidently has little difficulty in discovering all manner of predispositions in the guise of so-called location factors. Thus, the rise of new high-technology growth centers in the US Sunbelt is often said to be a result of such factors as the presence of an international airport, military bases, government research institutes, a major university with active science research programs, a high proportion of engineers and scientists in the local population, the availability of venture capital, abundant recreational resources, and so on. I have no intention of claiming that these factors are of *no* importance in the emergence of new high-technology growth centers, but I do want to suggest that the simple locational factors approach as such is deeply flawed, for the mere listing of the raw attributes of any given place (even those attributes endowed with some real locational effectivity) can never in and of itself provide definitive insights into the mechanisms of economic development that *over quite long periods of time* keep the engines of industrial growth running. In practice, explanatory exercises based on the enumeration of locational factors usually degenerate into nothing much more than the drawing up of bills of specifics that seem curiously tailored to fit each individual case.

With this cautionary note in mind, I hope to demonstrate in this and the next chapter that we can often best understand the evolutionary dynamic of localized production complexes (especially those formed, and forming, in the context of the new regime of flexible accumulation) in terms of an unremitting *endogenous* logic of the division of labor and (via external economies of scale) the formation of intense agglomeration economies. This logic is operative with varying degrees of force in industrial growth centers no matter what the specific stimulus behind their initial developmental spark. To accomplish the analytical goal of revealing the inner workings of this logic we must first of all deal with some basic issues in the theory of industrial organization. In what follows, these issues are presented at a high level of abstraction that for the most part cuts across the historical and geographical specificities of particular regimes of accumulation.

The scale and scope of the firm
Firms are able to expand or contract along two principal dimensions. One dimension is represented by scale or quantity of output; the other is represented by a series of aliquot functions (for example, spinning, weaving, dyeing, machinery repair, accounting, and so on) that firms may or may not internalize within their spheres of operation. The actual evolutionary path followed by any firm relative to these two basic dimensions is in large degree structured by internal economies of scale in the first case, and internal economies of scope in the second.

Suppose that a given firm produces a single homogeneous output whose quantity is denoted by x. For illustrative purposes let us call this output 'spun yarn'. The total *average* cost of producing yarn at level x is given by the function $f(x)$. Economies of scale are present wherever any increase in x leads to a decrease in the value of $f(x)$; and conversely *dis*economies of scale are present wherever an increase in x is followed by an increase in $f(x)$. More generally, economies of scale are said to exist if for any given value of x there is another value, say x' ($x < x'$), such that $f(x) > f(x')$. Over the long run, under conditions of economic competition, the firm will tend to exploit all its internal scale economies and produce x at a level that minimizes $f(x)$.

Take now the case of a second industrial activity, for example the weaving of cloth, which uses yarn as an input. Weaving may be vertically integrated with spinning (that is, spinning and weaving are combined within a single firm) or it may be vertically disintegrated (spinning and weaving are carried out in independently owned establishments). In the case where weaving is vertically disintegrated from spinning, we define its average production cost as $g(y)$, where y is the total output of cloth. In the case of a vertically integrated spinning and weaving firm we write the joint average cost of production (in terms of cost per unit of cloth) as $h(x, y)$. Let us assume for simplicity and without any loss of generality that one unit of yarn forms the input for one unit of cloth (that is, the physical input – output coefficient linking the two activities is unity) and that, under conditions of vertical integration, x and y are always produced in equivalent quantities. This latter assumption will be relaxed at a later stage. We can now roughly, and as a first approximation, define economies of scope as existing when we find the inequality

$$f(x) + g(y) \geqslant h(x, y) \, .$$

Wherever this condition prevails for specified values of x and y, vertical integration of the two activities will tend to occur. Where we find the converse case, we say that *dis*economies of scope are present, and this suggests that the two activities will be vertically disintegrated. The above remarks apply, mutatis mutandis, even where the jointly produced outputs have a purely conglomerate relation to one another, that is, where there is no input–output connection between them. However, for the remainder of this analysis, questions of conglomerate production organization will be relegated strictly to the background.

In general, scale effects in production have their basis in technological and organizational indivisibilities; and scope effects have their basis in the positive and negative transactional relations that are established in the interstices between different units of productive activity. Of immediate analytical importance is the manner in which the scale and scope effects defined above are intertwined with one another in the actual functioning of economic production systems. The interplay between these effects can be deciphered with the aid of the graphical model laid out in figure 3.1 which deals with two different activities whose levels of output are, again, defined by x and y, respectively. In order to clarify the meaning of this figure, I have broken it down into three separate panels labelled (a), (b), and (c). Let us consider each in turn.

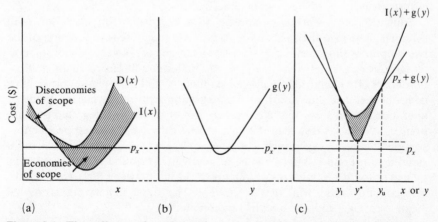

Figure 3.1. The effects of scale and scope on the vertical organization of production. The optimal solution is vertical integration. Definition of symbols: $I(x)$ average cost curve of x under conditions of vertical integration; $D(x)$ average cost curve of x under conditions of vertical disintegration; $g(y)$ average cost curve of y; p_x market price of x.

Panel (a) shows two average cost curves, $I(x)$ and $D(x)$, and a price line p_x. The curve $I(x)$ represents a possible average cost schedule for the production of x under conditions where this activity is vertically integrated with the production of y. $D(x)$ is the average cost curve for x where the two activities are vertically disintegrated. Both curves exhibit typical variable scale effects. In some cases the production technologies underlying the curves $I(x)$ and $D(x)$ will be identical, and in other cases they will differ; here, for the sake of argument, we may assume them to be different. For ease of exposition (and without any loss of generality) all scope effects within the firm are simply and arbitrarily defined relative to given quantities of x. We can now thus identify economies and diseconomies of scope in purely quantitative terms as $s(x) = D(x) - I(x)$. By this definition, economies of scope prevail where $s(x)$ is positive and diseconomies of scope prevail where $s(x)$ is negative. In figure 3.1, it is presumed that scope effects are themselves dependent on the scale of production, and here they are shown—arbitrarily—as rising from diseconomies to positive economies as values of x increase. If output x is produced in vertically disintegrated form, then it will be sold to producers of y through a system of market transactions at the unit price, p_x. As indicated in figure 3.1, this price will in the long run coincide with the minimum point on the average cost curve $D(x)$. For simplicity, we may take it that the value of p_x includes any *external* transactions costs involved in shifting x across intermediate market institutions.

Panel (b) of figure 3.1 simply indicates the average production cost curve, $g(y)$, for the second activity. Note that, even though economies and diseconomies of scope are dependent on the interaction between the two activities, these are not shown here as they have all been assimilated into the cost structures already laid out in panel (a).

Panel (c) represents a composite view of production costs for both activities. The average cost of joint (vertically integrated) production of the two outputs is shown as $I(x) + g(y)$. The average cost of vertically disintegrated production is shown as $p_x + g(y)$, for, under conditions of disintegration, producers of y would simply purchase inputs of x at their market price. Now consider whether integration or disintegration will be the chosen mode of operation. We observe that the average cost of vertically integrated production, $I(x) + g(y)$, is less than the cost of vertically disintegrated production, $p_x + g(y)$, for values of y such that $y_l \leqslant y \leqslant y_u$, where the subscripts l and u stand for lower and upper bounds, respectively. Since the value of y (that is, y^*) that absolutely minimizes production costs lies between these two bounds, vertical integration will, in this example, be the efficient organizational solution for the production of the two commodities.

Suppose now that the curves $I(x)$ and $D(x)$ are readjusted relative to one another in such a way that economies of scope are greatly reduced (see figure 3.2). The net result of this change is that the average cost schedule for joint production, $I(x) + g(y)$, shifts upwards relative to the average cost schedule for vertically disintegrated production, $p_x + g(y)$. If the shift is large enough, this will eventually make vertical disintegration the optimal organizational solution for the production of the two commodities. This may be so, moreover, even if positive economies of scope make their appearance at some point [as they do, for example, in panel (a) of figure 3.2 at production levels in excess of x'].

The examples studied in figures 3.1 and 3.2 have been constructed in such a way that all average cost curves attain their minimum levels at approximately the same values of either x or y (recall that the physical input–output coefficient remains fixed at unity). Of course, in these two simple cases, the information given in panel (a) is already sufficient to determine the optimal organizational form of production. As we shall see, however, the situation rapidly becomes more complicated with variations in the shape of the average cost curves. Here, we need to deal with two important and contrasting possibilities.

First of all, let us consider the case where the optimal scale of production of x (whether under integrated or disintegrated conditions) is far below the optimal scale of production of y. This situation is depicted in figure 3.3 where economies of scope are now shown—again arbitrarily—as constant per unit of output. We shall continue to assume that x and y are produced in balanced proportions when vertical integration prevails. In this case, even with the presence of strong economies of scope, the optimal organizational solution for this example is vertical disintegration, for diseconomies of scale in the production of x just at the point where y attains its optimal level (y^*) would push joint production costs up to grossly inefficient levels. In fact, vertical integration is efficient in relative terms only up to the upper bound y_u in figure 3.3; beyond this bound it is cheaper for producers of y to purchase x on the open market at the price p_x. However, a series of other

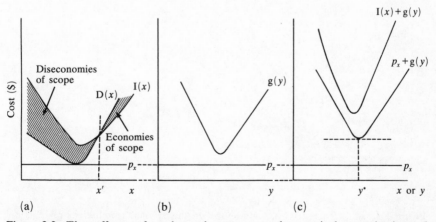

Figure 3.2. The effects of scale and scope on the vertical organization of production. The optimal solution is vertical disintegration. See figure 3.1 for definition of symbols.

organizational configurations now become evident as possible alternatives to the simple solution shown in figure 3.3. These would consist in integrating any number of single units for the production of x into the firm, running each at its optimal level x^*, and then, if necessary, either (a) making up for any remaining deficits of x by means of purchases on the open market, or (b) selling off any excess production of y. These different alternatives would be likely to engender some diseconomies of scope (perhaps because of the need for labor to manage the additional tasks of coordination), which might therefore reduce their attractiveness to the firm.

Second of all, let us examine the case depicted in figure 3.4 where the optimal scale of output for x greatly exceeds the optimal scale of output for y. In this figure, discrepancies in levels of optimal scale again make vertical disintegration the most efficient solution under conditions of balanced production levels for x and y, though, as before, innumerable alternative possibilities involving vertical integration are evident. Thus, in parallel to the previous case, y may be manufactured internally at its optimal level, y^*, in multiple production units, and any remaining mismatches between x and y dealt with by market transactions. Once more, these alternatives would be attractive only to the degree that they did not give rise to burdensome diseconomies of scope.

In the light of the arguments deployed above it is evident that scale and scope effects interact with each other in many different and subtle ways within the organizational structure of production. As a consequence, patterns of firms and markets constitute extraordinarily complicated fields of substantive possibilities. I have attempted to identify something of the

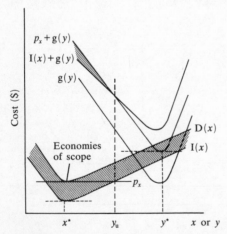

Figure 3.3. The effects of scale and scope on the vertical structure of production, with $x^* \ll y^*$.

logic of these possibilities by, in essence, combining elements of the important theories of vertical integration and disintegration developed by Stigler (1951) and Williamson (1975). Individually, these authors have certain blind spots, for the former deals only with the role of economies of scale in production, whereas the latter focuses on scope effects (seen as transactional costs and benefits) abstracted away from the effects of technology. Taken together and partially synthesized, as above, their analyses have considerably enhanced explanatory power. Alchian and Demsetz (1972) have proposed a yet different approach which emphasizes indivisibilities in production. This is a useful perspective for it points to the very real possibility of forms of technical change which resynthesize disparate production tasks into unified integrated machine systems, though we must also fully acknowledge the possibility of technical change in the other direction. Even so, the Alchian–Demsetz view is limited in range, for in fact vertical integration often occurs where clear technical separabilities exist, just as disintegration is at least a theoretical possibility even where technical unity prevails (for example, a chemical-processing plant broken down into materially-indivisible but separately owned segments, with metering of the flow-through in each segment).

As shown above, the problem of vertical integration and disintegration must take simultaneous account both of scale effects and of scope effects in the production process. The analysis is now ready for further generalization, and here I deal with the rather involved question of the wider systemic meaning of the vertical structure of production (or, in other terms, the social division of labor) within variegated complexes of production.

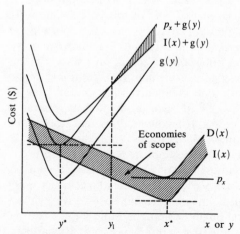

Figure 3.4. The effects of scale and scope on the vertical structure of production, with $x^* \gg y^*$.

The social division of labor: from the firm as an organization to organizations of firms

In neoclassical economic theory, the firm is characteristically treated as the embodiment of a production function in which inputs of capital (K) and labor (L) are transmuted into a quantity of output (Q) via a process defined in algebraic terms as $Q = \phi(K, L)$. The production-function approach describes the abstract quantitative relations between inputs and outputs (and is the basis for the neoclassical claim that income distribution is governed by marginal productivity), but it is strictly silent on two critical issues that turn out to be crucial to any understanding of what a firm is as a living social institution. These issues were first raised by Coase (1937) in an attempt to identify an alternative (institutional) theory of the firm. One concerns the organization of the firm as an internalized set of transactions linking its various parts into a managerially coordinated whole. The other concerns the organization of complexes of firms into networks of purely externalized transactional relations. These two issues raise a third critical question, namely, how is the boundary between the internal and external organizational structure of firms determined and how does it change through time?

In response to these problems Coase suggested the very general solution that a firm will progressively internalize transactions until the cost of organizing an extra transaction internally is equated to the cost of carrying out the same transaction externally on the market. To avoid possible misunderstandings here, it should be stated at once that the costs and benefits to the firm of the marginal transaction depend strictly on its current organizational configuration, and this further signifies that the firm's optimal transactional structure will rarely be achievable by means of simple stepwise expansion (or contraction) at the margin. In spite of this complication, we may usefully reinterpret Coase's solution (using the analytical language of the previous section) as signifying that firms will seek out internal transactional structures that balance scale and scope effects against market prices of inputs and outputs (where these prices include any additional transactions costs external to the firm). The great advantage of this way of treating the problem is that it allows us to seize production in general (a confusing assemblage of labor processes, technologies, physical stocks, and so on) as a coordinated system of internal hierarchies and external markets (Williamson, 1975). Better yet, since there is not in reality a sharp break between internal (hierarchical) and external (market) relations, but an irregular continuum extending over a variety of intermediate forms (joint ventures, partnerships, quasi-vertical integration, and so on), we can see production as a complex but rationally comprehensible organizational structure rooted in the polarities of the firm and the market (cf Richardson, 1972). This view is complementary to, and not in opposition with, those conceptions of production that strongly emphasize the tense force-field of capitalist – worker relations, for we must recognize that capitalists face not only the problem of pumping out surplus labor, but also the problem of securing the organizational conditions under which the surplus can be efficiently secured and productively redeployed in new investments.

Thus, from an organizational point of view, production consists of units of vertically integrated hierarchical order separated from one another *in a social division of labor*. Inside the firm, transactions are subject to managerial authority and are ultimately ruled by fiat. In external markets, transactional relations are governed by price signals. In intermediate, quasi-hierarchical or quasi-market settings, transactions are subject to more complicated rules of order, including various kinds of power relations, as, for example where technology exchanges, licensing agreements, long-term and medium-term contractual engagements, and so on are at stake (cf Taylor and Thrift, 1982). The situation becomes even more complicated when we take into account the circumstance that firms may, in addition, be spatially disintegrated into multiple discrete establishments, each of them with many independent external transactional relations.

Notwithstanding the complexity of these phenomena, it may generally be averred that, as vertical disintegration (the social division of labor) moves forward, so production systems become steadily more externalized and hence, in organizational terms, more flexible. Vertical integration, by contrast, signifies increasing organizational *in*flexibility for it puts limits on the possibilities for combination and recombination of individual production processes. A fertile terrain for the efflorescence of the social division of labor is an ensemble of economic sectors in which a multiplicity of different production tasks exist, some or all of which resist resynthesis into enlarged units of fixed capital, and whose effective coordination poses difficulties for management. Such industries run the gamut from clothing production to aerospace manufacture. Sometimes, but by no means always, the early innovative or intermediate stages of development of a new industrial ensemble (that is, when production technologies are experimental and unstable) are especially marked by this sort of multiplicity. Equally, however, other sectors evolve from a 'mature' vertically concentrated form into fragmented organizationally dispersed units, as emphatically demonstrated by Storper and Christopherson (1987) for the case of the Los Angeles film industry. More generally, the social division of labor between different units of production will tend to widen and deepen as the ratio of internal economies of scope to external transacting costs falls under identifiable scale conditions. But what, we might ask, are the concrete circumstances that are likely to give rise to this state of affairs? In practice, the variety of such circumstances would seem to be enormous, and a full enumeration of them—those that are empirically observable and those that are possible in principle—would be virtually endless. In spite of this difficulty, five important exemplary cases are of especial interest and significance for the analysis that follows.

First, then, fragmentation of production into an extensive division of labor is apt to occur where market conditions are unstable and uncertain as a result, say, of rapid fluctuations of demand or insistent product differentiation and competition. Firms will want to minimize the negative impacts of these conditions on their production schedules. Thus, to evade the transmission of costly production irregularities through an extended integrated chain of production, firms break up into fragmented units linked to one another via market (and quasi-market) transactions. This allows those producers who directly face final markets to raise and lower production levels rapidly by means of flexible upstream subcontracting and input purchases. At the same time, by the law of large numbers, the flow of economic activity through the system of subcontractors and input suppliers will always be more regular on average than the flow through any one vertically integrated channel. Disintegration signifies, then, that upstream producers will be able to achieve relatively stable output patterns, though at the cost of increased variability in external linkages.

Second, as figures 3.3 and 3.4 suggest, vertical disintegration may occur where interlinked production processes have widely varying optimal scales of operation. The tendency will be accentuated if internal scope effects are neutral or negative. For example, in the printed circuits industry, it is often found that small firms will subcontract out the tasks of drilling holes into circuit boards because they do not have the volume of output needed to keep an efficient numerically controlled drilling machine in full-time operation (see Scott, 1983). It is, moreover, generally inefficient in managerial terms for a limited number of printed circuits producers to internalize the drilling function while simultaneously attempting to commercialize excess capacity. By contrast, specialized drilling subcontractors can achieve internal economies of scale by pooling many different orders; at the same time, because they focus their managerial efforts on a restricted range of tasks, their production costs remain competitive.

Third, where external transactional relations are rendered immune from certain pervasive problems of market failure, disintegration will tend to ensue. As Williamson (1975; 1985) has shown, market failure in transactional relations can occur under a great variety of empirical circumstances, of which the following are of especial importance, (a) the monopolization of input or output markets, which destroys bargaining alternatives, (b) the presence of problematical firm-specific content in job orders, leading to difficulties of execution for those not properly educated in or sensitive to the nature of that content, and (c) irremediable inequalities in the amounts of information possessed by different parties to a given transaction so that one side can benefit at the expense of the other, as, for example, in the case of an independent research consultant who, with inpunity, withholds from a client useful findings generated in the course of carrying out the client's command. Some of these problems of market failure may be alleviated where large numbers of producers exist, where labor processes are routinized (even though tasks may be customized, as in the case of subcontract sewing operations in the clothing industry), and where communities of trust are formed in which customary norms of business are actively cultivated. The latter phenomenon would seem to be especially prevalent in centers of traditional craft industry (cf Ganne, 1983; Raveyre and Saglio, 1984).

Fourth, vertical disintegration is a common response to situations where segmented labor markets prevail. Firms that are ensconced in high-wage primary labor markets (often, in practice, large firms with unionized workers) will invariably find it to their advantage to subcontract out demands for unskilled work to firms employing low-wage secondary labor. By this means, they are able to limit spillovers of their advantageous employment conditions to a wider group of workers. Accordingly, many large firms in both North America and Western Europe today maintain subcontracting relations with either (a) local small producers employing immigrant and/or femaled labor, or (b) more distant producers, often in Third World countries, where wages are low and employment conditions inferior to those found in the core capitalist economies.

Fifth, and last, geographical agglomeration can also lead directly to vertical disintegration. With many different producers located in one particular area, search costs are lowered, business relations can be established and consolidated with relative ease, and the physical expenses of transport and communication are greatly attenuated. As a result, external transactions costs will fall, encouraging production processes to break institutionally apart.

In empirical circumstances where combinations of these inducements to vertical disintegration are actively at work, vigorous institutional fragmentation of production processes is to be expected. Moreover, if markets are also expanding, fragmentation can increase yet further. This particular point was argued out at length by Adam Smith in *The Wealth of Nations* (1776) where he showed that with increases in the extent of the market, new and increasingly specialized forms of production are able to emerge and to be maintained in full-time employment. To be sure, Smith was arguing here in terms of the *technical* division of labor within the firm, but as we know from the discussion above, under specifiable conditions of scale and scope, this technical division may break up into a *social* division of labor between firms. Moreover, insofar as extension of the market leads to an expanding social division of labor, we might refer to this as a process of *dynamic vertical disintegration*, for it concerns something much more than a simple institutional breaking apart of a given and invariable set of production activities. What is involved here is a process of disintegration *plus* innovation, so that, as the whole system expands, it acquires new and independent forms of specialized economic activity, but in a socially divided form. The extension of the market also encourages horizontal enlargement of the whole production system, by permitting the entry of more and more producers of a given type; and, under appropriate conditions (namely, reductions in optimal scale) *horizontal disintegration* may come about, that is, specifically, an increase in the number of individual producers for a given constant quantity of market output.

There is in principle no end to these processes of division, diversification, multiplication, and specialization in capitalist production complexes, though we must remember that they are not necessarily irreversible and there are in practice many cases where they can be seen to have been reversed. Where they are proceeding forward over time, the whole production system comes to form a network of interconnected activities with an intricate but identifiable organizational logic.

The organizational logic of industrial complexes

An industrial complex is, specifically, a large assemblage of producers tied into an interdependent whole by means of their external transactional relations. Observe that this definition stresses the functional and purely nongeographic qualities of the phenomenon; and not until the next chapter will the locational significance of industrial complex formation be considered. Just as single firms expand or contract along the dimensions of scale or scope, so complexes of firms expand or contract both along the vertical and along the horizontal axes of production organization (see figure 3.5). These dimensional variations bring into play a series of important system effects.

To begin with (and picking up on an earlier hint) an industrial complex marked by a deepening social division of labor is likely to be the organizational locus of considerable innovation. Not all industrial innovation consists in the relentless pursuit of aprioristic research programs by large and highly capitalized firms with specialized R&D departments. Much of it consists of small-scale entrepreneurial experimentation in organizational niches created by the expanding division of labor. Much, too, is born in the

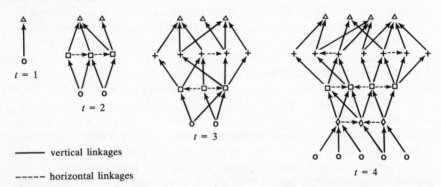

Figure 3.5. Vertical and horizontal expansion of an industrial complex, showing evolution of system from two establishments in two sectors ($t = 1$) to twenty-three establishments in five sectors ($t = 4$).

relational practices of firms where incremental problem-solving occurs at the external interface between suppliers and users of particular products. Thus, as Russo (1985) has indicated for the case of the ceramics production complex of Sassuolo, Italy, multiple minor innovations are continually being engendered at the interface between the specialized firms that manufacture machinery and equipment for ceramics production, and the users of that machinery and equipment who are constantly providing information feedback to the first set of firms. This sort of innovation is unobtrusive but immensely important in the unfolding of real industrial systems, and it is undoubtedly much in evidence in complexes that are expanding overall and simultaneously experiencing strong internal differentiation.

Because the growth of any complex also brings about combinatorial extension of the set of interfirm transactional possibilities, the organizational flexibility of the whole system tends by the same token to increase. Individual producers are able to build and rebuild external contacts with increasing ease and speed, which means that they can at the same time change their internal process and product configurations all the more readily. Even where individual production strategies are relatively rigid, the entire system itself is capable of supplying a wide range of outputs by means of varying vertical combinations of producers, and, in the same way, rapid changes in the design and quality of final products become an everyday possibility.

Last, the proliferation of increasingly more specialized producers in any given complex tends to result in continual reductions of the costs of production. Vertical disintegration is itself a response to the search for reduced costs and, as it occurs, producers perform their narrowing range of tasks with increasing intensity and efficiency. In addition, growth of the complex means that it is ever more easy to find competent specialist subcontractors who can take on important but infrequently performed production tasks. In short, the social division of labor leads to intensified 'roundaboutness' of production, and the net result is an everexpanding field of *external economies of scale* (Böhm-Bawerk, 1891; Young, 1928). These phenomena are likely to be one of the essential foundations of observed Verdoorn effects in growing economies, that is, rising industrial productivity as a consequence of expanding industrial output (Kaldor, 1970).

Each of these points reinforces the observation that it is simply self-defeating to attempt to conceptualize the process of production in capitalism simply in terms of the individual firm and its presumed behavioral proclivities. Production is a vastly more complicated phenomenon involving both the single enterprise (*qua* a vertically integrated structure of governance) and the interactive system or network of socially divided enterprises. Each single enterprise, to be sure, is an active element of the system, but no one enterprise can unilaterally control the social conditions of its own existence. These conditions are determined collectively within the entire social division of labor. By extension of this argument, it may be proposed that industrial technology itself is not just the simple hardware of production, but also the whole (internal and external) organizational disposition of the system enabling the hardware to function interactively and effectively.

This view of industrial organization puts considerable emphasis on the problem of transactional interrelations and forms of economic coordination. I suggest that investigation of this problem represents an especially critical prelude to location theory and geographical analysis generally. It constitutes an essential step in the analytical movement from macroeconomic models of capitalism to forms of spatial differentiation, and vice versa. In particular, this step informs us about some of the important specific questions that we must address in order to disaggregate the macroeconomic level into a set of particular geographical outcomes and then pack these together again into the totality of capitalism.

Our task is now to investigate the specific spatial order and rationality that characterize organized industrial complexes of the sort described here. This involves, above all, a study of the dynamics of locational agglomeration and of the formation of industrial communities.

Industrial localities

The generalized dynamics of industrial organization as described above give rise to a distinctive tendency for agglomerations of producers to arise at various locations on the landscape of capitalist society. These agglomerations coalesce out of the dense networks of transactional interrelations that form as the social division of labor deepens and as particular groups of producers are brought into intense and many-sided interaction with one another. But agglomeration, as such, is also in part an effect of the diverse local labor-market and community structures that come into being around any nucleus of industrial employment. All of these phenomena—groups of producers, local labor markets, and community life—interpenetrate with one another in intricate ways to form the concrete geographic reality of industrial localities.

Industrial linkages and agglomeration

We have already seen that any deepening of the social division of labor entails a widening of the external transactional structures (that is, linkages) of the production system. These linkages are by definition spatially extensive and they have strong but complicated locational repercussions depending on their precise physical and institutional characteristics.

External transactions between units of production may consist simply of physical input–output flows, as represented by the sale and purchase of material products; they may also assume the form of subcontracting arrangements in which work is done by one firm on behalf of another according to customized specifications; many transactions, in addition, are composed purely of intangible exchanges of messages and information in which firms make business arrangements, plan future actions, and monitor their economic environment. These various types of transactional activity are far from being mutually exclusive and, indeed, they overlap with one another to a considerable degree. All of them occur in a wide variety of institutional contexts (for example, spot markets, contractual agreements, part-ownership arrangements, understandings about reciprocity, and so on), and are mediated through many different transfer modes, depending on the nature of the exchange (for instance, road, rail, telephone, telex, mail, personal contact, and so on).

No matter what their form, institutional setting, or mode, all inter-industrial linkages incur costs that are a positive function of linkage length. There are several important dimensions to these costs. First, the unit costs of linkage are almost always inversely correlated with magnitudes of flow. Small flows are usually unable to generate strong economies of scale in the transfer process, and are thus more expensive in unit terms than large flows which can command significant discounts. Second, the physical variability of linkage flows also adds to their cost, for where the character of the flow changes constantly with respect to shape, weight, packageability, perishability, and so on, appropriate transfer arrangements cannot be economically standardized. Third, if linkages are unstable in terms of their spatial and temporal patterns, costs are likely to be high, for in this case linkage partnerships must be continually readjusted and the fixed costs of setting up and carrying out transactions incurred over and over again. Fourth, where linkages must be intermediated by face-to-face contact between one or more individuals their cost is liable to be especially high in view of both the time and travel costs involved. Fifth, and last, physical linkages consist of units of circulating capital that have a definite cost per period of idle time; increases in linkage length augment this cost by diminishing the velocity of rotation of the whole production system.

In circumstances where groups of producers have much interaction with one another that is expensive in the senses enumerated above (that is, where the interaction is made up of many small-scale, physically variable, and unstable transactions involving much personal intermediation, and with heavy time-dependent circulation costs) they are likely to condense in geographical space as tight functional clusters of activity locationally focused on their own center of gravity. In this manner, the linkage costs incurred in organized networks of vertically disintegrated producers may be sharply reduced in comparison with the case where the same producers are widely scattered over the landscape. Furthermore, as the velocity of rotation of the whole production system increases with intensifying agglomeration, so the need for producers to maintain buffer stockpiles of inputs or outputs is correspondingly diminished. This latter advantage of spatial agglomeration is being rapidly rediscovered at the present time as firms seek to reorganize production within the precisely modulated input–output structures of just-in-time delivery systems. Although any given spatial cluster of producers will be marked internally by strong transactions-intensive activity, it will also tend to have economic relations over a more extensive geographic area. By the same token, agglomeration is usually a response to the cost pressures of only a selected critical set of interestablishment linkages: not all (or even most) linkages of establishments in a given agglomeration will invariably be confined to the local area and, as already suggested, many establishments will also have connections on a wider national and even international scale.

Sometimes the core industries in a complex of tightly interlinked establishments depend strongly on inputs that cannot easily be moved across geographic space, for example coal or iron ore, or agricultural products. This was, of course, especially the case in earlier historical periods. In these circumstances, the complex as a whole may be expected to locate adjacent to a site where the relevant inputs can be readily obtained. By contrast, many kinds of industrial complexes have in practice few ties to specific external locational bases other than those that come into being as a function of their own gravitational implosion. In industrial systems based on mass production, this implosion tends to take the form of a spatial symbiosis between leading producers and their direct and indirect input suppliers and subcontractors. In more flexible industrial systems, where there is often no dominant set of propulsive leaders, agglomeration occurs simply as a consequence of the mutual attraction of each producer to every other producer in the complex.

In summary, then, increasing roundaboutness of production leads to increasing external economies of scale as expressed in system-wide reductions of production costs and increasingly efficient transactional arrangements. These external economies, however, frequently do not attain their final and most effective form until — as a result of the locational behavior of firms—they are translated into and consumed in the guise of agglomeration economies. Roundaboutness and agglomeration are also mutually reinforcing phenomena. Thus, on the one side, the social division of labor provokes spatial agglomeration as a way of lowering external transactions costs; on the other side, agglomeration encourages further social division of labor and in-migration of new producers precisely because it lowers these costs; and so the cycle of action and reaction continues until its inner energy is exhausted. Many centers of industry are in consequence exceptionally densely developed and much variegated in their range of economic activities. Tendencies to agglomeration are yet further underpinned where assemblages of producers make collective use of large indivisible infra-structural artifacts thereby reducing the cost of the latter to each individual user.

Local labor markets in industrial localities
The problem
With the rise of any industrial agglomeration, local labor markets are set in motion, and they too help to boost processes of spatial concentration and growth. As the employment base in any area increases, population tends to grow. Many different skills and economically useful human attributes are accordingly also brought into being in the area and sold on local labor markets. Regular structures of commutation join places of work and places of residence into a composite community whose overall geographical form is regulated by a series of interdependencies between wage rates, transport costs, and land rent (cf Scott, 1981). At the same time, the spatial pattern of the local labor market is subject to a number of cross-currents involving, above all, complicated processes of labor-market turnover and search. These processes are inscribed within what Clark (1986) has called the 'local class bargain', meaning a given balance of political and economic power between employers and employees on the factory floor as well as in the community at large.

All of these questions are of great intricacy, and it is certainly neither feasible nor useful to attempt to explore them exhaustively in the present context. Instead, I shall concentrate in what follows on the specific issue of instability in the external labor market as manifest in processes of turnover and search, for this has special relevance to any investigation of agglomeration economies under conditions of flexible production. At the same time, this instability is often accompanied in internal labor markets by a breakdown in institutional rigidities in the assignment of workers to tasks. The search for external and internal labor-market structures of these sorts (particularly in markets for secondary labor) is precisely one of the major reasons why flexible producers are so anxious to avoid unionization of their workers. It also helps to explain why secondary labor markets with high levels of flexibility (that is, instability) are generally dominated by politically marginal workers such as immigrants and women, for, as employers well recognize, these kinds of workers are likely to offer minimal resistance to erratic and insecure conditions of employment.

Labor-turnover processes

Increased labor turnover and accelerated job switching among workers is evidently a major sign in the external labor market of rising flexibility of the production system at large. As shown in the recent research of Scott (1984) and Storper and Christopherson (1987), this can affect workers in upper-income labor-market segments just as much as (and even occasionally more than) it effects those in lower-income segments.

Labor-turnover processes can be crudely dichotomized into accessions (new hires and recalls) on the one hand, and separations (quits and layoffs) on the other (see figure 4.1). In any one local labor market, accessions and separations will tend to follow broad seasonal and cyclical patterns, overlain by a purely random element. In a previously published case study of the labor-market activity of animated film workers in Los Angeles, I have shown how the recurrent and regular components of labor turnover tend to become internalized within workers' expectations as part of the 'normal' annual rhythm of work and unemployment (Scott, 1984). This internalization represents an important element of the local socialization and habituation of workers, for it helps to render the status quo legitimate and apparently unproblematical.

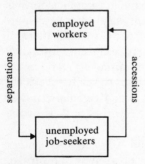

Figure 4.1. A simple labor-turnover cycle.

The purely random component of labor turnover consists of an amalgam of irregular and unpredictable decisions on the part of employers and/or employees to break or recreate anew the employment relation. Precisely because these decisions are irregular and unpredictable they will be likely to result in a balance between (the random components of) accessions and separations as the local labor market grows bigger. This balancing is a direct expression of the operation of the law of large numbers which tells us that the expected mean value of a sample of observations (accessions or separations) will converge asymptotically to a stable value as sample size increases. This suggests, in turn, that the larger the labor market, the greater is the likelihood that the mean random accessions rate and the mean random separations rate per establishment will tend to constant values. Moreover, since these rates are generated by the same stationary random process (a separation at one random time period equals an accession at another random time period) they will also tend to be equated to one another. The net result is that the buffer pool of unemployed job-seekers will itself become stabilized with increasing labor-market size, as can be inferred at once from the simple relationships sketched out in figure 4.1.

One corollary of the above remarks is that employers will be able to trade on the increased stability of average turnover and the pool of unemployed job-seekers as the size of the labor market increases. They are likely to do this by raising their own rate of turnover in an attempt to fine-tune over time their employment of labor with their need for work done, for the larger the labor market, the more sure they can be of finding workers to hire as soon as they are needed. The diminished search costs associated with large labor markets, as will be shown below, further encourages a policy of accelerated labor turnover. By the same token, workers are able to move from job to job with increasing ease and rapidity as the local labor market increases in size.

A testable hypothesis that emerges from these remarks is that, after abstracting away from the effects of cyclical and seasonal rhythms, we should find a positive correlation between labor turnover and size of local labor market. Another way of expressing the same idea is to say that workers in small labor markets are likely on average to experience longer periods of employment or unemployment whereas workers in large labor markets are likely to experience frequent and shorter bouts of employment or unemployment. In fact, Jayet (1983) has found this to be exactly the case in his recent econometric study of French local labor markets.

Labor-market search patterns in spatial context

In general, increased labor turnover promotes greatly increased search activities on the part both of workers and of employers in the labor market. The extent of these activities is sometimes reduced by the emergence and formalization of temporary layoff and recall procedures (so that workers remain attached to the same employer through periods of unemployment), but increased investment in labor-market search activities is nevertheless the usual counterpart of rising turnover. Thus, at any given moment of time in any local labor market, numbers of job-seekers will be looking for employment, just as numbers of employers will also be seeking to fill job vacancies. The tasks of matching prospective employees and prospective jobs involves two stages. First, active search is necessary (both on employees' and on employers' sides) in order to reveal the possibility of a match. Second, some further investigation will usually be necessary (perhaps an interview) to ensure that (a) the employer's conditions of labor are satisfactory to the job-seeker, and (b) the job-seeker's qualifications (including subtle but important behavioral and social attributes) are acceptable to the employer. If the second stage results in a failure, the search process then proceeds over again.

Labor-market search activities like these are likely to be highly developed in labor markets built up around flexible production systems. They are costly to all participants and the longer they endure, the more expensive they become, not just in terms of direct costs, but also in terms of benefits foregone, that is, lost production and wages. Nonetheless, they are at least to some extent made more efficient as the size of the local labor market increases, for, in general, information itself is more easily diffused in large as opposed to small labor markets (cf Stigler, 1962). The latter proposition may be clarified by reference to figure 4.2. Assume that we have three local labor markets labelled a, b, and c in ascending order of size. Let us define the expected total gains from search (either to a worker or to an employer)

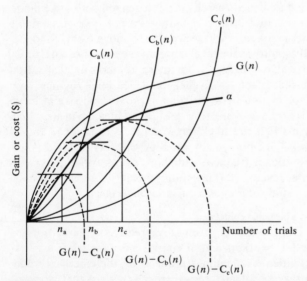

Figure 4.2. Expected gains from job search and costs of job search in three different local labor markets, a, b, and c; n_a, n_b, and n_c represent the optimal number of trials in each market, respectively.

as the function $G(n)$, where n represents the number of trials in the search process. The function $G(n)$ increases monotonically with n. It is assumed for simplicity that $G(n)$ is identical for all three local labor markets; in reality, $G(n)$ would be likely to be correlated positively with size of labor market, though inclusion of this refinement in the analysis would only further strengthen the argument that now follows. Let $C_a(n)$, $C_b(n)$, and $C_c(n)$ be the total costs of search as a function of n in each labor market, with unemployment rates, for simplicity, held constant throughout. These costs follow the ordering $C_a(n) \geqslant C_b(n) \geqslant C_c(n)$, because the greater the size of the labor market, the more information at the margin a given effort of search is likely to yield; for example, in a larger center a newspaper advertisement will reach a wider audience, a trip to a labor exchange will provide a longer list of possible openings, or a door-to-door enquiry will continue to reveal new possibilities even after extended prior enquiries.

In any one local labor market, the optimal number of trials in the search process is defined on average by the value of n that maximizes net gains, that is $G(n) - C(n)$. Behavioral sequential search models provide more elaborate criteria of optimality than this (cf Phelps, 1973), but the present rough formulation is adequate for present purposes. Given the shapes of the curves $G(n)$, $C_a(n)$, $C_b(n)$, and $C_c(n)$ in figure 4.2, it is evident that (a) for any given value of n, the expected gains from search will increase with increasing labor-market size, and (b) search will tend to be more prolonged in larger labor markets because this will bring expected additional benefits. Note, in particular, that the curve labeled α in figure 4.2 traces out a locus of points representing optimal net returns to search for labor markets of different sizes, and this curve rises steadily upwards as we move from smaller to larger markets. The evident deduction is that labor-market search and job-matching processes will tend to become more efficient with more insistent spatial agglomeration.

Flexibility in local labor markets

These analyses of labor turnover and labor-market search suggest that the familiar notion proposed by Oi (1962) that labor constitutes a quasi-fixed factor of production, must be to some extent adjusted for labor-market size. Labor is fixed or quasi-fixed only to the degree that it is irreplaceable, and, if we hold the level of firm-specific human capital constant, its irreplaceability diminishes relative to the size of the local labor market. This follows from the earlier argument to the effect that it is always on average easier to fill a given job vacancy in a large labor market than in a small labor market. The consequence is that we would definitely expect to find employers in densely concentrated industrial centers relying more frequently and to a greater degree on the external labor market than employers at more isolated locations (abstracting away from occupation and sector, of course).

On a series of different counts, then, the rotation of workers through any given localized job system is likely to be a direct function of the overall magnitude of the system, on condition that the size of the total job pool, and the number of unemployed job-seekers remain in constant relation to one another. As it happens, we may predict that large labor markets will have higher unemployment rates on average than small ones because the superior probability of finding employment there (even if for relatively short periods of time) is likely to induce in-migration of a proportionately greater number of job-seekers. In partial confirmation of this proposition, Sirmans (1977) and Vipond (1974) have both shown that urban unemployment rates tend to increase with city size. The net result of all this is that the flexibility of local labor-market arrangements will tend to increase as a positive function of size. This also suggests, again, that flexibility in terms of production organization and flexibility in terms of employment relations will intersect with and reinforce one another in particular localities. Moreover, on the basis of studies by such researchers as Brusco (1983), Garofoli (1983a; 1983b), Hall (1962), Hoover and Vernon (1959), Solinas (1982), and Vernon (1960), among many others, we know that labor-market flexibility in dense industrial districts with many disintegrated secondary firms is frequently raised to yet higher levels of development by reason of the patterns of part-time and temporary work, double job-holding, home-work, illegal work arrangements, and employment of adolescents and even of children, that are prevalent in many such districts.

Community life and social reproduction in industrial localities
Industrial localities are something very much more than simple foci of economic production. They also represent durable human communities in which, with the passage of time, particular traditions and forms of culture accumulate. This community aspect of industrial localities is obviously deeply important, but also immensely difficult to summarize succinctly. Even if there were well worked-out theoretical investigations of particular aspects of community life in industrial localities, the degree of idiosyncrasy and local color that obtrudes in each specific instance would still make meaningful discussion troublesome to organize. I shall therefore do no more here than to sketch out a few background notions that seem to be especially useful for understanding the detailed case studies that follow in chapters 5, 6, and 7. A fuller comprehension must no doubt come in large degree from intensive historical and geographical investigations of ways of life in particular places at particular moments of time.

The growth and internal diversification of any industrial agglomeration will cause it to draw into its orbit increasing numbers and varieties of workers. These workers are invariably housed in residential areas accessible to major workplaces. There ensues at once a potentially explosive predicament whose resolution depends on social and political mechanisms that lie far outside of the production system in the narrow sense. On the one hand, the production system engenders and supports a variety of different skills and occupational categories within the local labor force. On the other hand, the intermingling in urban residential space of individuals who differ widely from one another in these respects is frequently a source of rising social tensions. In the modern high-technology industrial growth centers of the Sunbelt, for example, sharply segmented local labor markets have tended to come into existence comprising highly qualified managerial and technical cadres on the one hand, and unskilled, often immigrant, workers on the other. These two groups mix closely together in the workplace, but are inclined scrupulously to avoid one another in the wider sphere of social life. One of the ways in which this avoidance is expressed is in forms of residential behavior that actively bring socially segregated neighborhoods into being. Patterns of social and spatial segregation are then boosted to yet higher levels of resolution by land-use controls, building ordinances, and planning legislation that seek to protect higher-status neighborhoods from invasion by lower-status households.

The socially specialized neighborhoods created in these ways are generally distinguishable from one another by reference to the broad patterns of occupational and socioeconomic stratification prevailing in the community at large. In this manner, certain aspects of the division of labor in the production system become reexpressed, imperfectly and with many distortions, but nevertheless identifiably, in a variegated social division of community space. One of the useful attributes of this division of community space is that it helps to achieve smooth reproduction of relevant occupational and socioeconomic categories by promoting cultural homogeneity of the primary domain in which family life, interpersonal exchange, and leisure-time activities are situated. The division of labor in production and the social division of community space are thus in part reflections of one another, and each is in some way enhanced by the functioning of the other. These relationships become more clear and effective with increasing community size, which allows for the disaggregation out of ever more diverse patterns, including some (for example, those based on religion or life-style) that have no direct connection to the production system as such.

Each community is a repository of attitudes, habits, forms of consciousness, and so on, interpenetrating with local structures of work and life and thickening over time in response to the expansion of collective historical experience. One aspect of these subtle but important processes was captured by Marshall (1920; 1932) in his account of the formation of industrial districts in which he points to the impregnation of the very atmosphere of the community with the mysteries of local trades which forthwith become "no mysteries". More specifically, tangled informal networks of useful knowledge about local production methods, business conditions, and employment practices are an intrinsic element of community consciousness and help to keep the whole system functioning smoothly. Personal knowledge of others in the community becomes an essential component of the ways in which the local economy operates. As indicated in the previous chapter, small producers in traditional craft centers seem to depend to a major degree on the familiarity and trust that are generated in the business community over time [cf Ganne (1983) and Raveyre and Saglio (1984) for their studies of such communities in France, and Becattini (1987) and Fuà (1983) for their comments on the Italian case]. Workers, too, learn to navigate skillfully through the complexities of their workaday existence, and, because of their intimate knowledge of local production activities and opportunities, many become entrepreneurs in their own right, often at the outset by starting up a small subcontract shop.

Educational institutions in the local area also add their weight to the general process of social reproduction in line with prevailing business needs and labor-market trends. Teaching and research programs are frequently adjusted explicitly to local conditions. Hence, for example, we find that schools and universities in Detroit have an inordinately high proportion of activities related to the car industry; in Los Angeles to the film and aerospace industries; in Manchester and Leeds to textiles; and so on. Probably the most celebrated case of this symbiotic relation between educational and research activities on the one hand and the local production system on the other, is Stanford University with its science and engineering programs closely tailored to the needs of nearby high-technology firms in Silicon Valley. Contrary to the views expressed by some analysts (for example, Rogers and Larson, 1984), who seem to see Stanford University as a sort of external independent variable in the growth of Silicon Valley, I suggest that the relationship, both in this specific instance and more generally, should be seen as one of mutual interaction and interdependent development.

In any industrial locality, then, complex and socially useful patterns of socialization and community development tend to evolve, enlarging the entire stock of agglomeration economies, and thus, in many direct and indirect ways, helping to reduce the private costs of production. However, the communal experience of workers can also be a double-edged sword for producers. The dense presence of many individuals in both the workplace and the home-place facilitates political mobilization and—with many local variations to be sure—diverse kinds of labor organizations and groups of community activists may come into existence. In general, workers build up a certain comprehension of their class and communal being, and accordingly they also learn ways of collectively confronting threats to their interests on these fronts. In the old centers of Fordist mass production in North America and Western Europe, such forms of political solidarity have in the past stood in the way of many different claims and initiatives on the part of employers, and accordingly they have also partially compromised agglomeration economies. Even had there been no threats from foreign competitors over the 1970s and 1980s, it is likely that rising worker opposition (combined with intensifying agglomeration *dis*economies in such matters as congestion, pollution, the inflation of land values, and so on) would still have provoked a considerable degree of organizational and technological restructuring in the mass-production system and a concomitant steady outflow of productive capital.

Conclusion
From all of the above, it is apparent that the geography of agglomerated production complexes in contemporary capitalism (and particularly in the regime of flexible accumulation) poses innumerable problems. Effective analysis of these problems demands, at a minimum, an examination of the elaborate interplay between many small-scale and large-scale forces. On the one hand, processes of vertical disintegration and interlinkage induce spatial agglomeration at particular sites, which then also become foci of intricate local labor market and community processes. On the other hand, there would also seem to be a tendency for these sites to swarm within extensive spaces or regions offering broadly positive sociocultural conditions for production. Moreover, important shifts in the character of this interplay may be expected as the regime of accumulation changes. Concrete examples of these propositions can be found in (a) the growth of Fordist assembly industries in the large cities of the US Manufacturing Belt in the interwar period, (b) the recent emergence of the Third Italy with its panoply of artisanal production centers, or (c) the expansion of flexible high-technology industries in the new growth centers of the contemporary Sunbelt. This manner of approaching an understanding of industrial geography intentionally downplays the idea that it is analytically meaningful or useful to focus attention on attempts to identify pregiven locational factors underlying the rise of each individual complex of producers. It may well be that certain of these factors do occasionally help to pinpoint particular locational outcomes, but their theoretical interest is frequently of minor importance compared with the issues discussed above. These issues, to repeat, revolve around the evolutionary logic of the industrial system and its associated local labor markets, and the endogenous dynamic of growth and development that this logic sets in motion.

It should be added that the economic and social activities described in this chapter give rise in each particular industrial community to extremely diversified forms of local history and geography. As suggested earlier, any attempt to summarize these forms of history and geography in a generalized theoretical statement would in all likelihood do much violence to our understanding, though this is certainly no reason why we should not attempt to abstract out from them particular systematic issues and subject them to analysis. In the end, no doubt, significant comprehension of industrial communities, new and old, must be based on dense monographic description of specific cases combined with generalized theoretical scrutiny. In other words, we want, at one and the same time, to be able to keep in sight the obvious and important differences between, say, the modern craft communities of the Third Italy and the new high-technology growth centers of the

US Sunbelt, while simultaneously acknowledging that there are likely to be important common processes operating in both situations. One of the central themes of this book is that the logic of flexible production, as reflected in technologies, organizational patterns, and labor-market structures in the new industrial spaces of North America and Western Europe, represents just such a set of common processes.

The Third Italy: industrial tradition and renaissance

In what has gone before, I have discussed a number of basic processes underlying the formation of agglomerated production centers in new industrial spaces under conditions where the social division of labor is particularly active. The recent ascent of flexible accumulation in the advanced capitalist societies has restimulated these conditions, leading at the same time to much industrial growth in areas that have hitherto not experienced extensive industrialization. In the present and the two

Figure 5.1. The administrative regions of the Third Italy.

succeeding chapters, I propose to carry out three major case studies of this phenomenon. These case studies do not in any sense represent formal systematic tests of the theoretical ideas described above; rather, they are illustrative examples—of considerable empirical interest and significance in their own right—demonstrating how some of these ideas can help us understand the locational unfolding of flexible production systems in contrasting social settings.

I begin with an account of the recent rapid industrial development of the Northeast and Center of Italy—the so-called Third Italy. For present purposes, this area is defined as comprising the seven administrative regions of Emilia-Romagna, Friuli-Venezia Giulia, Marche, Trentino-Alto Adige, Tuscany, Umbria and Veneto (see figure 5.1). This entire area has grown rapidly over the last couple of decades on the basis of a profusion of labor-intensive and socially fragmented industries, many of them with deep historical roots in local artisanal traditions. Many of the characteristic features of the Third Italy are also observable in parts of the neighboring regions of Abruzzi, Lazio, and Lombardy.

Regional development in Italy since World War 2
Three Italies
Over much of the period since the Second World War, regional development theorists have typically described the Italian space-economy in terms of a simple bipartite split between the North and the South, that is, on the one side, the highly developed area of the Industrial Triangle defined by Genoa – Milan – Turin, and on the other side, the backward Mezzogiorno. The first area is preeminently a zone of large metropolitan regions focused on a series of major growth poles comprising industrial sectors such as basic chemicals, cars, electrical appliances, and shipbuilding, most of which are organized along mass-production lines. The Mezzogiorno, by contrast, is still strongly agricultural in character, though since the early 1960s it has been steadily invaded by large capital-intensive branch plants controlled from the North. These branch plants have on the whole failed signally to foster local developmental effects (cf Dunford, 1988).

Throughout the period of vigorous Fordist and neo-Fordist accumulation coinciding with the long postwar boom, this bipartite developmental pattern dominated the entire economic geography of Italy, and was generally considered to represent the underlying coordinates of all probable future lines of expansion. In this context, the Northeast and Center of the country was for the most part simply either overlooked, or else was assimilated into the North as a relatively uninteresting territorial extension of the great productive region of the Industrial Triangle. In the same way, such features of the manufacturing system as subcontracting and the artisanal firm were widely regarded as archaic and vanishing residuals from the past (Michelsons, 1985).

For the greater part of the present century, the Northeast and Center of Italy has functioned primarily as an agricultural area, with some urban settlement in a dense network of small and medium-sized towns. Industrial activity in these towns was largely confined to small firms producing outputs for local consumption, such as clothing, farm machinery, furniture, porcelain, shoes, textiles, and so on. In the 1950s this unpromising industrial base began to expand rapidly, and it continued to grow at an accelerated pace over the 1960s, and even over the 1970s and 1980s when most of the leading industrial sectors of the North were in the throes of crisis and recession.

Regional development theorists at first had some difficulty in coming to terms with the rapid industrial expansion of the Third Italy, and they certainly initially tended to depreciate its importance and originality. In many quarters, it was thought to be little more than a temporary and aberrant phenomenon, a side-effect of the economic crisis in the major industrial centers, and hence likely to recede into the background again once the mass-production system of the North was brought back to full economic health. Indeed, it was not until the path-breaking work of Bagnasco (1977) that the industrial development of northeastern and central Italy with its basis in the *fabbrica diffusa* (that is, the organizationally decentralized factory) was recognized as a durable and significant third alternative to the established patterns of industrialization in the North and South, and as the expression of a distinctive social formation in its own right.

The Third Italy in context
Since the Second World War, then, the Third Italy has undergone a remarkable transformation in which it has evolved from an industrially marginal area to one of the major foci of growth in modern Italy. Between 1961 and 1971, industrial employment in the Third Italy grew by 25.9%, whereas in the rest of the country it grew by only 11.8%. In the crisis years between 1971 and 1981, when, industrial employment in the rest of Italy expanded by only 4.3% (with a decline of 2.2% in the region of the Industrial Triangle), it increased in the Third Italy by as much as 19.7%. And by 1981 the Third Italy accounted for as much as 37.3% of the nation's total employment in manufacturing.

Figure 5.2 helps to put this growth in context. The figure provides information on aggregate patterns of industrial activity in the seven administrative regions of the Northeast and Center compared with the four regions of the North and the nine regions of the South. The figures show how changes in industrial employment, numbers of establishments, and average establishment size have occurred relative to one another for all twenty regions over the period from 1971 to 1981.

Figure 5.2(a) graphs out changes in industrial employment against changes in number of industrial establishments. The North, Northeast and Center, and South emerge at once as highly distinctive regional groupings on the basis of these variables. First, the regions of the North declined in terms of industrial employment between 1971 and 1981, but tended to make small gains in terms of number of industrial establishments. These trends in the North can be seen as the outcome of the crisis and concomitant restructuring of mass-production industries over the 1970s (as elsewhere in North America and Western Europe), along with some limited but definite growth of small firms on the pattern of the Third Italy (cf Garofoli, 1983a). Second, by contrast with the North, the regions of the Northeast and Center display vigorous growth on both dimensions, reflecting above all extremely rapid rates of new firm formation. Third, in the South, all regions show gains in

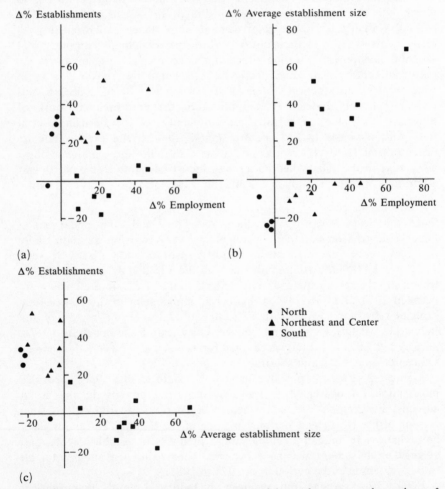

Figure 5.2. Italy: Percentage change in industrial employment and number of establishments, by administrative region, 1971–1981. Source of data: *Censimento Generale dell'Industria, del Commercio, del Servizi e dell'Artigianato.*

employment, though the total number of establishments tended to decrease over the designated time period. These trends in the South can be explained in terms of continued transfers of employment from the North to southern branch plants combined with the closure of many small firms in the South (cf Del Monte and Giannola, 1986).

Figure 5.2(b) shows changes in industrial employment relative to changes in average size of establishment. Here, we see that the North's loss of employment between 1971 and 1981 was associated with reductions in the average size of industrial establishments. This is consistent with a situation where some new small firm formation is also going on, thus accentuating, as a statistical phenomenon, decreases in average plant size. In the Northeast and Center, the observed *growth* of employment was accompanied by *declining* average establishment size, suggesting a very vigorous process of new firm formation indeed. The South gained in terms of both employment and average size of establishment, thus reinforcing the idea that its employment expansion was confined to existing (large) plants while small establishments tended to disappear.

Figure 5.2(c) conveys information already in essence revealed by figures 5.2(a) and 5.2(b). However, the figure also indicates that there is a strong negative correlation in general between changes in average establishment size and number of establishments for the Italian regions. The Northeast and Center of Italy emerges, once more, as an area of strong growth in numbers of establishments, with a tendency for the same establishments to become steadily smaller in size.

This preliminary description thus confirms the view of the Third Italy as a distinctive economic and spatial entity within the Italian regional system. In contrast to the experience of the major centers of mass production in the advanced capitalist societies during the 1970s, the Third Italy experienced rapid growth of industrial employment and high rates of new firm formation over the same decade. Moreover, all this was associated, significantly, with a tendency for individual units of production to become smaller in size. I shall argue below that these developments can be understood as the expression of an advancing social division of labor in highly competitive industries whose outputs are able to dominate an ever-widening circle of national and international markets.

The pattern of industrialization in the Third Italy and its socioeconomic foundations
The manufacturing base
The Third Italy today has an exceptionally diversified manufacturing base. Table 5.1 lays out employment statistics for the whole area cross-tabulated for twenty sectors and the seven administrative regions. The table omits information on (a) energy, gas, and water, (b) mining of metallic and nonmetallic minerals, and (c) building and construction, all of which are commonly included in compilations of Italian industrial statistics.

With the aid of simple location quotients, much useful information can be gleaned from table 5.1 about spatial patterns of industrial specialization in the Third Italy. The location quotient (q_i) is a simple statistic defined for the ith industrial sector in any given area as

$$q_i = \frac{\pi_i}{\pi^\star} ,$$

Table 5.1. Employment in manufacturing industry in Northeast and Central Italy, 1981. Source: *6° Censimento Generale dell'Industria del Commercio, dei Servizi e dell'Artigianato, 26 ottobre 1981.*

Code	Sector	Emilia-Romagna	Friuli-Venezia Giulia	Marche
22	Production and primary transformation of metals	5068	3722	2005
24	Processing of nonmetallic minerals	60638	6544	7248
25	Chemicals	19229	2054	3086
26	Artificial and synthetics fibers	282	1082	12
31	Metal products	78224	18583	14668
32	Machinery and mechanical equipment	91954	12765	8743
33	Office machines and data processing equipment	805	212	220
34	Electrical and electronic equipment	30639	16614	10024
35	Motor vehicles, motor bodies parts and accessories	13610	1293	942
36	Other means of transport	9902	7721	3638
37	Precision instruments and apparatus; medicosurgical, optical and related instruments; clocks and watches	5602	2705	607
41	Basic foods	34547	4782	5727
42	Sugar, drinks, and other alimentary products; tobacco	17647	3554	4374
43	Textiles	39416	6868	7674
44	Hides and leather	6596	1798	4786
45	Shoes, clothing, and household fabrics	52907	5563	70904
46	Wood and wooden furniture	36692	30183	27496
47	Paper, printing, and publishing	20594	5917	5621
48	Rubber and plastic products	17484	2092	6496
49	Miscellaneous	6954	1188	8708
Total		548790	135240	192979

where π_i is the proportion of all industrial workers in the area employed in sector i, and π^* is the proportion of industrial workers in the whole country employed in the same sector. The location quotient is thus a measure of relative spatial incidence normalized to unity. It can now be used to determine which industries are underrepresented and which are overrepresented in the Third Italy as a whole, where underrepresentation is here defined for sectors with $q_i \leqslant 0.8$ and overrepresentation is defined for sectors with $q_i \geqslant 1.2$.

Table 5.1 (continued)

Trentino-Alto Adige	Tuscany	Umbria	Veneto	Total NEC	Italy	NEC q_i [a]
5117	17964	7852	8704	50432	197415	0.68
3276	36032	8624	37766	160128	319341	1.34
2113	18749	4720	21853	71804	264057	0.73
392	349	1551	1720	5388	28812	0.50
8240	35540	8787	76271	240313	705290	0.91
4798	21131	4764	50385	194540	502455	1.04
88	696	62	904	2987	36392	0.21
5853	19326	2755	34253	119464	481927	0.66
3994	6239	923	6004	33005	273953	0.32
286	18972	1555	12736	54810	139370	1.05
1433	3683	749	10913	25692	68894	1.00
4213	14693	4907	23806	92675	263550	0.94
2570	7097	4812	11338	51392	140556	0.98
3021	82096	8761	54453	202289	493423	1.10
449	21551	677	15343	51200	86078	1.59
3472	92531	15382	103529	344288	636231	1.45
13230	41058	6820	73057	228536	447790	1.37
4346	18038	3634	25731	83881	274003	0.82
2605	10552	1425	20843	61497	211870	0.78
1464	12483	565	12394	43756	100650	1.16
70960	478780	89325	602003	2118077	5672057	

[a] See text for definition.

By these definitions, underrepresented sectors in the Third Italy are
(a) the production and primary transformation of metals, (b) chemicals,
(c) artificial and synthetic fibers, (d) office machines and data-processing
equipment, (e) electrical and electronic equipment, and (b) rubber and
plastic products. These sectors are typified to a significant degree by
capital-intensive mass-production technologies and by the search for
internal economies of scale in individual units of production. Overrepresented sectors are (a) processing of nonmetallic minerals (ceramics and
pottery for the most part), (b) hides and leather, (c) shoes, clothing, and
household fabrics, and (d) wood and wooden furniture. These are all industries that tend to be labor-intensive and for which external economies of
scale are often much more important than internal economies of scale.
It may be noted that a number of industries mentioned in table 5.1 do not
yield high location quotients for the Third Italy as a whole but do nonetheless occur in important locally specialized concentrations within the area.
Two of these are of especial interest, namely the machinery and mechanical
products industry of Emilia – Romagna (along with the metal products
industry that provides it with critical inputs), and the textiles industry of
Tuscany. The first industry is engaged primarily in the production of
agricultural and industrial machinery, and the second in the production of
woven and knitted woolens. Once again, both are rather labor-intensive and
highly dependent on external economies.

The conditions of growth
What, we may ask, are the conditions that have helped to sustain this
distinctive and highly differentiated pattern of industrialization in the Third
Italy? Here, I shall first of all treat some general background issues of
geography and society in the Third Italy, and in the next section, I shall deal
with a number of more detailed questions about the organization and
location of industry in the area.
    As shown earlier in chapter 2, the ending of the long postwar boom in the
late 1960s and early 1970s was associated in the advanced capitalist
economies of North America and Western Europe with a crisis of Fordist
mass-production industry and concomitant social and political problems in
the great manufacturing regions that had arisen on the basis of this species
of economic activity. Even though the worst of the crisis now seems over, the
mass-production industries of North America and Western Europe have
found it increasingly difficult to reestablish their former hegemony, and they
continue right down to the present day to remain under considerable threat,
notwithstanding their attempts to regain lost strength by means of innumerable
changes in technological structure, interindustrial organization, and labor
relations. Those economies that have shown significant resilience and powers
of recovery in the recent past have tended to be significantly oriented to newly
resurgent forms of flexible production in both manufacturing and service
provision, and Italy is no exception to this general observation.

While the economy of the Industrial Triangle has languished since the early 1970s, the small-scale industries of the Third Italy have grown apace. Moreover, in Italy, mass production never really developed historically to quite the same degree that it did elsewhere. Unlike the case of Britain, for example, where large-scale industrialization over the 20th century more or less destroyed previous craft traditions of production (by driving up the price of labor and by encouraging standardization of consumption patterns) Italy retained a significant artisanal sector, and nowhere more so than in the small and medium-sized towns of the Northeast and Center of the country. Therefore, as flexible accumulation came, over the 1960s and 1970s, to be an increasingly viable form of industrialization for Western capitalism, the Third Italy had, as it were, a head start. Its traditional industrial communities with their fund of craft skills provided a basis on which the economic development of the area could move rapidly ahead. Its development has been consolidated by the fine quality of much of its industrial outputs, marked as they are by high levels of design intensiveness. This has enabled producers in the Third Italy to penetrate specialized market niches and to ward off competition from outputs originating in the world periphery. Development has also been to a significant degree underpinned by the creation of large-scale marketing and export organizations with aggressive international sales strategies.

The distinctive social formation of the Third Italy has, in addition, constituted a propitious environment for growth. On the one hand, the area remains relatively free from the militant forms of workerist culture and consciousness that are to be found in all of the large industrial communities of the North and that have engendered a long history of labor agitation in the large assembly plants of the latter area. On the other hand, and unlike the South with its semifeudal agricultural legacy, the northeastern and central part of Italy has for long harbored a spirit of small-scale entrepreneurial activity based on its traditions of urban artisanal production and its dominant sharecropping system of agriculture in which the returns to the sharecropper's labor have always depended strongly on an ability to make clear-sighted decisions and on the quality of work performed (cf Brusco, 1986). To be sure, many parts of the Third Italy are predominantly to the left of the political spectrum, and some flourishing municipalities (such as Bologna) have communist-dominated governments. If anything, however, left-wing municipalities in the Third Italy have tended to view small 'nonmonopolistic' industries with considerable sympathy and actively to encourage their local implantation. In any case, there is limited class polarization in the Third Italy between employers and workers, for both characteristically share a common social background. Many workers become small entrepreneurs, and failed entrepreneurs typically fall back into the ranks of the workers, so that class positions tend to be rather fluid. Moreover, a positive culture of work has been widely remarked upon as one of the prevailing attributes of workers in the Third Italy (cf Michelsons, 1985).

The typical features of local labor markets, too, in the Third Italy, have added their part to the industrial renaissance of the area. Following the Second World War there was a large reservoir of commercializable skills in the area, as well as a significant pool of surplus agricultural labor available for employment in local urban communities. Even today, many of the industrial workers of the Third Italy maintain links to farming (whether through ownership of a small-holding, or by means of customary attachments to a family farm, or by engaging in casual agricultural labor), and by this means they are often able to supplement their incomes. This in turn helps to keep wages down, just as it enhances the overall flexibility of the lower end of the labor market by encouraging part-time work among unskilled factory hands. Homework, as well, was and is prevalent throughout the Northeast and Center of Italy. For example, as Brusco (1982) has pointed out, some 50% of all the workers in the area of Modena and Reggio nell'Emilia (an area producing predominantly ceramics and clothing) are homeworkers. The institution of homework enables producers to tap reserves of cheap female labor that would otherwise not be available for employment on a regular basis within the factory; and it also provides a mechanism for evasion of health and retirement payments by employers. Where firms employ fifteen or fewer workers they are exempt from the legal obligations of the *Statuto dei Lavoratori* which codifies union rights in the plant, and this exemption operates over much the greater proportion of firms in the Third Italy. Many workers are in the habit of holding two jobs, at least one of which is likely to be in the underground economy. All this labor-market activity is kept in a high state of flux by the constant stream of information about job opportunities, employment conditions, and the like, that flows through the intricate social networks that are an intrinsic feature of community life in the Third Italy.

In this context of small family firms, diminished class polarization, and vigorous entrepreneurial energies, a number of specialized industrial agglomerations have grown rapidly over the last couple of decades. The vitality of these agglomerations as centers of production is sustained by the general sociogeographic conditions described above, as well as by hyperactive processes of vertical and horizontal disintegration and the concomitant creation of powerful external economies of scale. We now turn our attention to these latter issues.

Organizational and locational dynamics of industry in the Third Italy
Industrial geography of the Third Italy
The outlines of the industrial geography of northeastern and central Italy are depicted in figure 5.3, which shows all communes in the area with 750 manufacturing establishments or more. In drawing up this figure, I have selected establishments rather than employment as the operative measure of industrial development because the objective is to indicate not just the major industrial agglomerations in the area, but also the extreme institu-

tional fragmentation of production. Prato with its 9022 manufacturing establishments (mainly in the woolen textile industry) is by far the largest center on this criterion, followed by Bologna (6456 establishments concentrated in the metal and machinery industries) and Florence (6272 establishments in a mix of industries producing clothing, furniture, leather, and shoes). The three core regions of Emilia–Romagna, Tuscany, and Veneto clearly stand out as the main bases of industrial development in the Third Italy.

Within this overall area system, local specialization of production activities is extremely marked. In addition to the cases of Prato, Bologna,

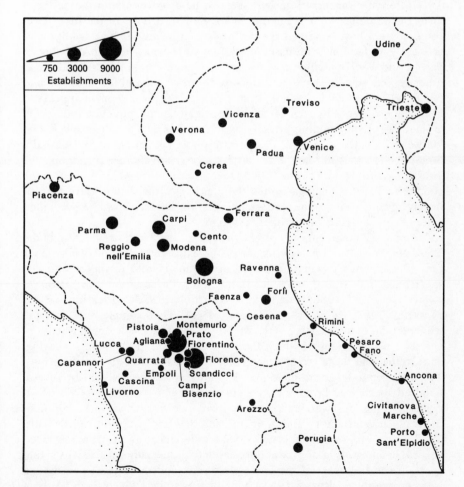

Figure 5.3. Third Italy: Communes with 750 manufacturing establishments or more, 1981. Source of data: *6° Censimento Generale dell'Industria, del Commercio, del Servizi e dell'Artigianato, 26 ottobre 1981*.

and Florence noted previously, the following examples of specialized industrial agglomerations may be cited (note that not all of these agglomerations
are large enough to make an appearance in figure 5.3): Arezzo (gold
jewelry), Carpi (knitwear), Castelfidardo (musical instruments), Montebelluna
(ski boots), Pesaro (furniture), Piacenza (buttons), Porto Sant'Elpidio
(shoes), Sassuolo (ceramics), and the list could be extended a dozen times
over (cf Garofoli, 1981). In centers like these, production is commonly based
on a rather incongruous mix of traditional labor-intensive skills and modern
computerized and microelectronic technologies (Piore and Sabel, 1983).

Social divisions of labor and spatial agglomeration

Two different moments of genesis seem to be discoverable in the development of the industrial agglomerations of the Third Italy. In the first place,
some centers have emerged on the basis of a centuries-long tradition of
artisanal production. The cases of pottery in Faenza, food processing in
Parma, and woolen textiles in Prato are exemplary here. In the second place,
other centers seem to have developed only within the last few decades, and
in a purely spontaneous fashion. In many cases, this development appears to
have been triggered by spin-off from a prior isolated production unit, or by
a plant closure stimulating workers to go into business for themselves. The
knitwear industry of Carpi, design-furniture production in Bassano del
Grappa, and shoes in Marche are all cases of relatively recent spontaneous
growth according to Brusco (1986) and Fiorentini (1983). Whatever the
conditions that may have attended the planting of the seed of development
in any given instance, the important question here is how the seed then
emerged into a flourishing industrial system.

Virtually all commentators on the process of local industrialization in the
Third Italy insist on the significance of the extreme social division of labor
that characterizes production in the area and its role in the creation of
specialized industrial districts (cf Balestri, 1982; Becattini, 1987; Brusco,
1986; Cenzatti, 1986; Fuà, 1983; Garofoli, 1983a; Mezzino, 1985;
Mossello, 1987; Russo, 1985; Zacchia, 1984). For example, in Prato, the
woolen textile industry is vertically disintegrated into a multiplicity of
specialized operations of which the most important are spinning, weaving,
and dyeing, and these are complemented by dozens of additional functions.
The organizational coordination of the industry is accomplished by several
hundred specialized brokers or dealers (*impannatori*) who themselves do no
manufacturing but who successively farm out particular tasks to independent subcontractors and then market the finished product (Balestri,
1982). In the ceramics industry of Sassuolo, there is also an advanced
vertical disintegration of production, and most especially between firms that
specialize in the firing of the basic tile biscuit and those that specialize in
glazing operations (Russo, 1985). This then permits efficient high levels of
product differentiation in ceramics production at stages close to the final
market. The shoe industry of Marche is similarly deeply fragmented into

diversified subsectors and is, additionally, associated with a large number of different kinds of support services (Agostinelli et al, 1983). Once again, these examples might be multiplied at length by reference to various other industrial districts in the Third Italy specializing in outputs such as clothing, furniture, jewelry, leather goods, scientific instruments, and so on. At the same time, there is frequently in many districts (for example, Carpi, Sassuolo, Prato) a pronounced symbiotic division of labor between producers of the dominant local specialty on the one hand, and makers of the machinery and equipment used by those producers on the other.

In conformity with the theoretical notions laid out earlier in this book, this sort of functional disintegration can be seen in part as a primary cause of industrial agglomeration, and in part an outcome of that same agglomeration. Polyvalent industrial complexes made up of many different specialized producers tend to have dense and highly variable transactional relations running through them. Geographical agglomeration is a means of reducing the spatially dependent costs of these transactions and of accelerating the flow of semifinished products (circulating capital) throughout the system. The resulting industrial districts have been described by

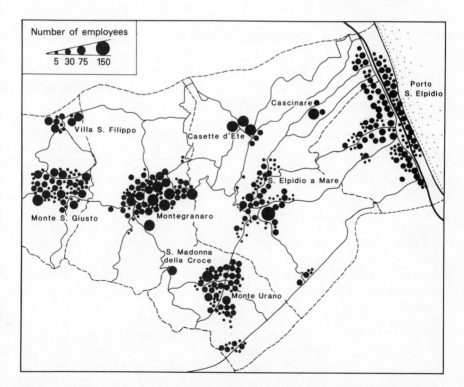

Figure 5.4. The locational structure of the shoe industry in the area of Porto S. Elpidio, Marche. Redrawn from Agostinelli et al (1983, figure 5).

Becattini (1986, page 27) in the following terms:

> "The technical separability of the different phases of production, the changeability of intermediate demands, the territorial contiguity of producers, and the harmony between the socio-cultural environment and established forms of manufacturing give rise to *a continuous flow of economies external to the single firm but internal to the industrial district* thus allowing the population of firms to renew itself and to grow continuously."

These external economies, when reinforced by the spatially polarizing effects of local labor markets provoke intense agglomeration of producers. An example of just how pronounced the phenomenon of agglomeration can be is shown in figure 5.4 which depicts the locational structure of shoe producers in and around the town of Porto Sant'Elpidio in the region of Marche. Here, hundreds of small producers, many with fewer than five employees, cluster tightly together along with suppliers of innumerable specialized services in half-a-dozen subcenters constituting a composite shoe-manufacturing district. This district alone produces two thirds of Marche's shoe exports and one quarter of the total national output of shoes (Cooke, 1987).

The superstructural environment of the industrial district

Frequently, in the industrial districts which emerge in the manner described above, various superstructural organizations also spring into being as a means of providing coordination and steering mechanisms, thereby consolidating localized agglomeration economies. Public and private organizations both perform these functions. Thus, on the one hand, nonprofitmaking collectives of producers sometimes form in order to supply specialized business-service functions that individual firms cannot profitably provide for themselves. Such services as accounting, materials purchasing, marketing, technical consulting, and so on, are often made available in this way in particular industrial districts. On the other hand, these same sorts of functions are also sometimes supplied by private profitmaking firms on the open market or by means of quasi-vertical integration between groups of interdependent firms. Thus, a dense network of private buying offices in Florence intermediates between much of the light industry of Tuscany and world markets (cf Becattini et al, 1983; Becattini, 1986). In the same way, the Benetton company acts as an intermediary between some 10 000 workers in independent clothing factories in the Third Italy, and 2000 franchised retail outlets all over the world, with computerized daily tallies of sales and subcontract orders flowing backwards and forwards through the firm's headquarters in Treviso (cf Murray, 1985).

Private and public marketing agencies of these kinds have been a crucial factor in the economic development of the Third Italy. They have provided a conduit through which the myriad small producers of the area have been able to dispose of their output on national and international markets. They have also facilitated extension of the market to a degree that has encouraged the extraordinarily high degree of vertical disintegration described above.

In 1950, as King (1985) has shown, Italy exported just 150000 pairs of shoes; by 1980, it was exporting shoes at an annual rate of 285000000 pairs. The effects of such explosive growth are immediately detectable in the burgeoning industrial districts of the Third Italy, and in the intense internal variegation of their industrial systems (cf figure 5.4).

One of the more remarkable cases of the superstructural business organizations that have come into existence in parts of the Third Italy is the recently inaugurated SPRINT project (Sistema Prato Innovazioni Technologiche), a private–public partnership devoted to the development of interindustrial telematics in the Prato woolens district. This is an attempt to reconstitute much of the transactional activity in the local economy of Prato on a telematic network based on a central computer and adjoining data banks. The project involves manufacturers, subcontractors, brokers, banks, local governments, labor organizations, and others, all linked together in the network to which access is gained by means of individual terminals. In this manner, the different participants in the industrial economy of Prato can send and receive information and utilize the system's data banks, and this will undoubtedly much enhance the efficiency of their external transactional relations. For example, through the SPRINT system, a manufacturer will be able to find out which subcontractors of a given type have capacity currently available at what price, or will have immediate access to up-to-date information on banking operations and local business conditions.

Early indications are that the SPRINT project has encountered a number of difficulties, especially among smaller enterprises who are reluctant to participate because of a perceived loss of business confidentiality. In principle, however, the project certainly represents a novel and powerful means of enhancing external economies of scale. It represents, potentially, a sort of advanced nervous system in the corporate body of producers, and if it can be made to succeed it is likely to boost considerably local productivity levels. In one form or another, versions of the system will assuredly make their eventual appearance in other major industrial complexes around the world, whether spatially polarized or not. Experiments with a similar kind of telematic project have indeed been reported in the textile center of Herning in Denmark. An interesting but rather speculative question at this point is whether and to what degree telematic systems like the Prato SPRINT project will in the long run dilute the strength of some kinds of agglomeration economies while (by encouraging further social division of labor) intensifying the strength of others.

The superstructural organizations characteristic of the industrial districts of the Northeast and Center fade at one extreme into what is widely referred to in the Italian literature (following Marshall) as 'industrial atmosphere' (cf Becattini, 1979; Bellandi, 1986; 1987). The term refers to the wider institutional, social, and cultural environment within which production actually occurs, and it is frequently a critical moment in the overall socioterritorial reproduction of any given industrial district. In particular, individual centers of production often develop deeply rooted cultural traditions in which practical knowledge about local trades and forms of business is unselfconsciously absorbed by the local citizenry. The process is reinforced where nearby schools and colleges provide specialized training suitable for local needs. Even peculiar linguistic conventions and vocabularies make their appearance—and this seems to be especially the case in Italy—thereby facilitating exchanges of information between the participants in the local economic system. The whole represents a world of learning by doing, of the irregular accumulation of practical knowledge and information, and of constant minor experimentation. By the same token, it is also a world in which industrial innovations and new business ventures tend to occur in profusion, but on a small and barely noticeable scale as they are secreted in the interstices of the organizational structures engendered in the daily practices of production and work.

Perspective on the Third Italy
The Third Italy is a unique combination of the new and the old. Advanced electronic technologies, often installed in family firms, exist side-by-side with sweatshops and homeworkers. Small labor-intensive enterprises in traditional centers of production participate in telematically based information systems. Age-old skills are deployed in fabricating products that are highly competitive on international markets. Cooperative interactions of a kind that might be thought to have been more common in an earlier era of stable craft communities subsist alongside cutthroat competition. Above all, the Third Italy represents probably the strongest revival anywhere in the advanced capitalist economies of North America and Western Europe of a pattern of industrialization—disintegrated artisanal production in specialized districts— that is reminiscent of a much earlier period of captialist development.

On these foundations, Italy has advanced in the 1980s from a position of relative industrial laggardliness to one of considerable dynamism in terms of growth and development, and the Northeast and Center is in the forefront of this shift. Indeed, when all the informal and underground elements of the economy are fully accounted for, the gross national product of Italy actually now surpasses that of Britain. Italy currently occupies fifth place in terms of gross national product among the Western nations after the United States of America, Japan, West Germany, and France. And much of this recent success is based on the exceptionally vigorous local economies of the Third Italy.

The economic model that has been set in motion in the Third Italy has many structural characteristics in common with the new flexible forms of industrial development in localized agglomerations now coming into being in many different parts of the world, as, for example, (a) in Europe, in such places as central Denmark, Flanders, Bavaria, southern and eastern England, or (b) in many different parts of the US Sunbelt with its burgeoning high-technology growth centers, or (c) in the major metropolitan regions of Southeast Asia with their rapidly expanding electronics production complexes. The Third Italy, however, is certainly one of the most original and advanced cases of the recent proliferation of agglomerated flexible production complexes. If flexible accumulation is, in fact, one of the important future paths of capitalist development, the lessons of the Third Italy will undoubtedly in due course come to be seen as being just as important as those of Japan.

6

The Scientific City, Ile de France South: the spatial logic of an emerging technopole

The Third Italy has risen as a major industrial force on the basis of design-intensive forms of manufacturing producing a diversity of consumer goods. This represents one kind of new industrial space within the emerging regime of flexible accumulation. Another kind, now developing strongly in many parts of North America and Western Europe, is founded on high-technology industrial sectors with significant R&D inputs. In France, such spaces have started recently to form in a number of different places. However, by far the largest of all the new French high-technology industrial regions is the expanding technopole of the Scientific City (*La Cité Scientifique*) located in the southern quadrant of the Ile de France (see figure 6.1). One of the particularly interesting aspects of the economic growth of this region is the highly visible role that a variety of governmental and quasi-official agencies have played in the consolidation of its positive attributes as a focus of industrialization.

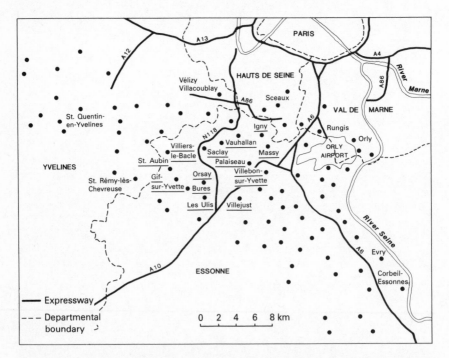

Figure 6.1. The Scientific City, Ile de France South. Dots represent centers of eighty-seven communes composing the City; selected centers are named. Communes with names underlined form the core area of the Scientific City.

Some preliminary definitions

The term 'Scientific City' signifies two rather distinctive and contrasting things. First of all, it designates a purely organizational entity in the form of a nonprofitmaking association devoted to promoting the development of the southern portion of the Ile de France. Second, it also designates a loose aggregate of some eighty-seven communes as identified in figure 6.1. There is no legal or administrative connection between the first and the second significations.

The Scientific City Association as such was founded in November 1983 with the support of the French government, local planning agencies, and various business corporations. Its primary objective is to function as a medium of information exchange between the different public and private institutions in the south of the Ile de France. It has no fixed geographical demarcation except for a broad but unofficial association with the general area shown in figure 6.1. This area includes the eighty-seven communes alluded to above, and these are taken as the specific, though arbitrary, territorial definition of the Scientific City for the purposes of the present investigation. This definition coincides with the one given in the Noë report that preceded the official constitution of the Scientific City Association (Noë, 1982). In figure 6.1 a *core area* is also identified comprising thirteen communes at the very heart of the Scientific City and constituting its functional and spatial center.

The geographical setting

The eighty-seven communes that make up the Scientific City proper represent a band of territory roughly 50 km long by 12 km wide stretching from the new town of St Quentin-en-Yvelines in the west to the new town of Evry in the east. The City lies mainly in the *département* of Essonne, but it also spreads over into the *départements* of Hauts de Seine, Val de Marne, and Yvelines. The northern fringes of this band of territory overlap with part of the inner suburban ring of Paris (*la première couronne*), though the greater portion of the Scientific City lies in the outer suburban ring (*la deuxième couronne*). The Scientific City thus abuts onto two distinctive geographical zones, namely, (a) in the case of the *première couronne*, an area that grew rapidly in the first half of the present century as a center of mass-production industries (in sectors such as cars, aircraft parts, machinery, and electrical goods) and that is today relatively heavily urbanized, and (b) in the case of the *deuxième couronne*, an area that retains considerable tracts of open space and agricultural land despite much recent urban development.

Notwithstanding the dense industrial and urban development of that part of the *première couronne* which lies adjacent to the Scientific City, it never became quite as heavily colonized by factories as the northern and northwestern inner suburbs of Paris (Bastié, 1964). Nor did it develop to anything like the same degree a heavy industrial base with strongly negative external effects on the local environment. At the same time, the part of the *deuxième couronne* that coincides with the Scientific City retains, as already pointed out, large areas of unspoiled greenery with considerable amenity value, and these areas are now strongly protected by vigorous planning legislation (CSAU, 1986). The entire region of the southern Ile de France has thus considerable appeal as a residential zone, and much of it, especially its core area, is occupied by managerial cadres, professionals, technocrats, and other intellectual workers. Indeed, since the 1930s, the main suburban commuter rail line stretching southwards and southwestwards from the Latin Quarter of central Paris through Massy, Palaiseau, and Orsay, to St Rémy-lès-Chevreuse has been a conduit for the residential dispersal of much of the teaching and research staff of the universities, laboratories, and *grandes écoles* concentrated in that part of Paris (Castells, 1975). When the French government embarked on a program of deconcentration and decentralization of these same institutions after the late 1960s, the area of the Scientific City was designated as a privileged recipient of them. In addition, an abundant supply of blue-collar labor suitable for employment in routine manufacturing activities is available in the two new towns at the eastern and western extremities of the Scientific City. The area also has a major international airport at Orly, and it offers much available land at moderate prices while remaining easily accessible via excellent road and rail connections to the multifarious business and governmental functions of Paris.

The Scientific City thus possesses many of the attributes that are often thought to be propitious for the development of high-technology industry. And, indeed, as some elements of the preexisting manufacturing system in the southern portion of the Ile de France (especially in the inner suburbs) began to evolve into modern high-technology forms of production, so they gravitated more and more strongly to areas in and around the Scientific City. More recently, the active and expanding entrepreneurial energies of the region have also brought considerable new high-technology industry into the area. Thus, today, the industrial base of the Scientific City comprises a rich complement of firms in such sectors as biotechnology, computers, electronics, instruments, machine tools, robotics, and pharmaceuticals, as well as an array of various low-technology industries. Despite these developments, the attributes of the Scientific City enumerated above by no means constitute the basis of a one-way developmental path into accelerated modern high-technology industrial growth. They have most certainly facilitated that growth, and they may in certain respects have helped to spark its genesis. However, they do not in any final sense account for the long-run developmental dynamic of the Scientific City as an evolving industrial system with an intensifying endogenous logic of growth. In order to understand that logic in its fullness, it is necessary to review the record of development of the Scientific City in the light of the theoretical arguments presented in chapters 3 and 4. I begin this task by sketching out some of the basic human and institutional resources that have recently accumulated in the area. I then follow this up with a detailed account of the changing patterns of industrial organization and location in the region as its economy shifts increasingly into flexible high-technology forms of production.

Population, education, and research in the Scientific City

One of the important manifestations of the recent industrial development of the Scientific City has been the rapid growth of its population along with a notable expansion in a series of local educational and research institutions. In conformity with the ideas expressed in chapter 4, these phenomena may be seen as representing basic conditions for the growth of modern industry; at the same time, they are themselves partially outcomes of that very same growth. Let us consider their overall development and structure.

Population

The Scientific City had a total population of 1 168 000 in 1982, as against a population of 933 000 in 1975—an overall expansion of 25.2% in just seven years. Over the same period, the total population in the two *départements* of the southern inner suburbs of Paris (that is, Hauts de Seine and Val de Marne) changed by a factor of − 2.9%. By way of comparison with two major US high-technology growth centers, the Scientific City is about 60% the size of Orange County (with a population of 1 933 000 in 1980) and it is virtually the same size as Silicon Valley (whose population was 1 291 000 in 1980).

The spatial distribution of the population of the Scientific City is shown in figure 6.2. Here, and subsequently, the study area consists not only of the

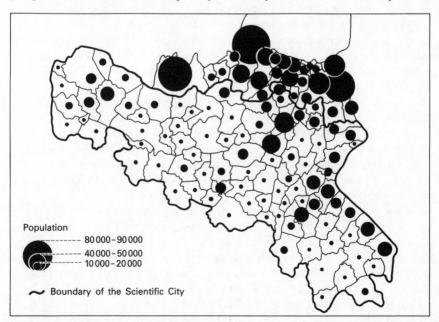

Figure 6.2. Geographical distribution of population by commune, 1982. Source of data: *Recensement Général de la Population de 1982.*

eighty-seven communes comprising the Scientific City proper but also, for comparative purposes, of a belt of suburban communes belonging to the *première couronne*, and lying between Paris and the Scientific City proper. Observe the steady and predictable decline in population density from north to south over this entire area. In the Scientific City itself, population is widely scattered, though with localized concentrations, namely, (a) along its older northeastern and eastern edge with a southward prolongation (passing through the new town of Evry) to Corbeil-Essonnes, (b) towards its western extremity around the new town of St Quentin-en-Yvelines, and (c) in the core area of the City. This core area is further distinguished by the unusually high proportion of scientific and technical workers in the general population, whereas residential areas in the eastern and western fringes of the City tend to be of lower socioeconomic status.

The Scientific City thus has a large and differentiated population representing a significant reservoir of labor. The overall spatial fluidity of this reservoir is continually being augmented by expanding investments in commuter rail and road transport facilities. That said, many large employers in the area have faced persistent labor shortages in the recent past, and several of them have attempted to deal with this problem by providing private bus service for their low-wage workers (Peyrache, 1984).

Education and research
With its major university, more than 60% of France's *grandes écoles*, and 43% of the nation's scientific research institutes and laboratories, the Scientific City is exceptionally well-endowed with a basic infrastructure of technology research and training establishments. These have helped continually to upgrade local skill levels and to disseminate locally useful technical information, thus contributing significantly to what was alluded to in the previous chapter as 'industrial atmosphere' with its subtle but deeply significant positive attributes for producers. Figure 6.3 displays the locations of some of the more important of these establishments in both the Scientific City proper and the southern inner suburbs of Paris. Note that the establishments referred to in figure 6.3 represent only a selected set of centers out of a much larger population of both public and private institutions in the study area. It has been suggested by Decoster and Tabariés (1986) that there are over 35 000 researchers now working in the Scientific City.

A particularly dense concentration of educational and research centers may be observed in the core area of the Scientific City, focused on the commune of Orsay and aligned along the scenic Chevreuse Valley with its major commuter rail connection to central Paris. Among other important facilities, the area contains the Commissariat à l'Energie Atomique at Saclay, the University of Paris South (with its strong concentration on the physical sciences) at Orsay, and the Ecole Polytechnique (the most prestigious of all French engineering schools) at Palaiseau. In this core area is to

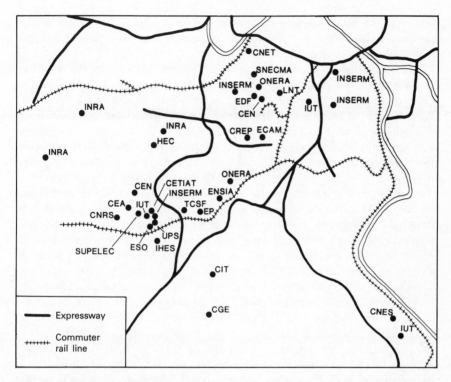

Figure 6.3. Major scientific/technical educational and research centers. Interpretation of acronyms:

CEA	Commissariat à l'Energie Atomique
CEN	Centre d'Etudes Nucléaires
CETIAT	Centre Technique des Industries Aéroliques et Thermiques
CGE	Compagnie Générale d'Electricité
CIT	Centre International du Téléphone
CNES	Centre National des Etudes Spatiales
CNET	Centre National d'Etudes de Télécommunications
CNRS	Centre National de la Recherche Scientifique
CREP	Centre de Recherche et d'Etudes Pharmaceutiques
ECAM	Ecole Centrale des Arts et Manufactures
EDF	Electricité de France (Etudes et Recherches)
ENSIA	Ecole Nationale Supérieure des Industries Agricoles et Alimentaires
EP	Ecole Polytechnique
ESO	Ecole Supérieure d'Optique
HEC	Ecole des Hautes Etudes Commerciales
IHES	Institut des Hautes Etudes Scientifiques
INRA	Institut National de la Recherche Agronomique
INSERM	Institut National de la Santé et de la Recherche Medical
IUT	Institut Universitaire de Technologie
LNT	Laboratoire National de Télécommunications
ONERA	Office National d'Etudes et de Recherches Aérospatiales
SNECMA	Société Nationale d'Etudes et de Construction de Moteurs d'Avion
SUPELEC	Ecole Supérieure d'Electricité
TCSF	Thomson-CSF (Centre de Recherches)
UPS	Université de Paris Sud.

be found an extraordinary assemblage of scientific/technical knowledge centers, surpassing by far similar concentrations in many US high-technology growth regions.

The gathering together of so much research activity in the southern reaches of the Ile de France is first and foremost the result of a series of decisive governmental initiatives seeking to ensure the deconcentration and decentralization of many of the public services that were formerly over-whelmingly located in Paris (cf Brocard, 1981; Cooke, 1985). Beginning with the implantation in 1949 of the Centre d'Etudes Nucléaires at Saclay, the planned shift of educational and research centers to the area accelerated over the 1960s and 1970s as policies to limit the growth of central Paris were elaborated and implemented with increasing determination. By the mid to late 1970s, it was becoming evident that these policies were also in practice bringing into being a major new pole of scientific and technical activity, and some commentators even began to speak optimistically, but somewhat prematurely, about the emergence of a French Route 128 in the vicinity of Orsay (cf Noë, 1982). Now that the area is also growing rapidly as a focus of industrial employment, many of these research centers are starting consciously to adjust their internal activities and external contacts to the commercial needs of the complex. However, as will be shown below, the level of interaction between public research institutions and industry in the Scientific City remains, even today, rather more restricted than might perhaps be expected given the insistence in much academic writing on the importance of such institutions for the growth of high-technology industrial regions (cf Dorfman, 1983; Rogers and Larson, 1984). Because levels of interaction are in fact so low in the Scientific City, the matter has now become an object of official concern and intervention.

Industrial development and structure of the Scientific City
Functional and spatial characteristics

The broad industrial structure of the entire southern sector of the Ile de France (that is, the four *départements* that meet on the terrain of the Scientific City) is displayed in table 6.1. In this general area, electrical and electronic equipment production is by far the major employer, and indeed, the Paris region as a whole is the privileged focus of the electrical and electronics industry in France, with some 40% of total national employment (FIEE, 1985). The second major employer in the area is road vehicle production, followed by machinery, parachemical products[1] and pharma-ceuticals, and naval and aeronautic construction. The pattern of industrial employment in the Scientific City proper would seem to be a fairly faithful reflection of the general sectoral structure laid out in table 6.1, though food-processing (or agro-alimentary) industries are also an important sector of

[1] Parachemical products include matches, glues, soaps and detergents, paint and varnish, photographic products, perfumes, and so on.

production, many of these being closely associated with the wholesale vegetable market serving the Paris region at Rungis (cf CSAU, 1985; Davoine et al, 1985).

Table 6.1. Employment in manufacturing industry in the southern Ile de France by *département* and sector, 31 December 1985, level 40A of the French standard industrial classification. Source: *Effectif des Salariés 31 décembre 1984*, II—*Les Départements de la Région d'Ile de France* Paris (GARP, 1985).

Code	Sector	Essonne	Hauts de Seine	Val de Marne	Yvelines	Total
T02	Meat and milk products	867	2486	1602	1157	6112
T03	Other agricultural and food products	5978	9763	7432	4500	27673
T04	Solid mineral fuels and coke	–	108	–	–	108
T05	Petroleum and natural gas	22	8703	246	32	9003
T06	Electricity, gas, water	533	857	14	703	2107
T07	Ferrous ores and metals, primary steel	17	1347	705	555	2624
T08	Nonferrous ores, metals, semimanufactures	26	1554	405	132	2117
T09	Construction materials, miscellaneous minerals	913	2376	1592	3112	7993
T10	Glass	526	1074	1112	61	2773
T11	Basic chemicals, artificial threads, etc	604	6288	3525	620	11037
T12	Parachemical products and pharmaceuticals	4312	26433	8157	3033	41935
T13	Foundries and metal working	4933	15029	8512	4489	32963
T14	Machinery	6937	16440	10575	8584	42536
T15	Electrical and electronic equipment	21332	61245	12818	27327	122722
T16	Road vehicles	2523	47494	2200	31322	83539
T17	Naval, aeronautic construction, armaments	7398	21430	1095	10959	40882
T18	Textiles and clothing	1086	3633	2286	822	7827
T19	Leather and shoes	336	450	532	88	1406
T20	Wood, furniture, and miscellaneous industries	1955	3464	3187	2881	11487
T21	Paper and cardboard	2002	2096	1321	720	6139
T22	Printing, newspapers, publishing	4607	12395	6305	2891	26198
T23	Rubber and plastic materials	1475	3435	1447	2518	8875
Total		63882	248100	75068	106506	498056

The industrial development of the southern portion of the Ile de France is thus based on a mixture of high-technology and low-technology production activities, representing in part different periods of suburban expansion and economic growth. As the empirical studies of Davoine et al (1985) and Peyrache (1984) demonstrate, most industrial employment in the region is still concentrated in the inner suburbs. However, in the 1970s and 1980s, many of the older industries in the inner suburbs were subject to much restructuring and considerable numbers of jobs were lost as a result (Husson, 1979). By contrast, since the late 1960s, the Scientific City proper has been a zone of overall industrial expansion (Guieysse, 1983; Peyrache, 1984). In 1983 total industrial employment in the City (including employment in building and public works) amounted to 102 225, representing a growth of 7.7% over the situation in 1976.

A preliminary view of the industrial geography of the study area is given by figure 6.4 which identifies the locations of all manufacturing establishments in the area with 1000 workers or more. There are thirty one of these establishments in total, all of them in just three sectors of production, that is, electrical and electronic equipment (which predominates by far), road vehicles, and aeronautic construction. Once more, the evident decline in density levels from north to south is apparent. In the Scientific City itself large manufacturing establishments are mainly ranged along its northern and eastern boundary areas with their relatively superior access to blue-collar labor. Two spatial nuclei stand out in particular, namely, Vélizy-Villacoublay which is the location of major establishments belonging to such firms as Avions Marcel Dassault SA, Citroën SA, Enertec SA, Matra SA, and SFENA (Société Française pour l'Equipement de la Navigation Aérienne), and (b) Evry/Corbeil-Essonnes with establishments belonging to Digital Equipment Inc., Hewlett–Packard Inc., IBM Inc., and SNECMA SA (Société Nationale d'Etude et de Construction de Moteurs d'Avion). Many of these establishments depend to a major degree, directly or indirectly, on French national defense expenditures. Most of them have important subcontracting linkages to firms in the local area as well as to firms in a wider national and even international sphere of operation (Bakis, 1977; CSAU, 1985). These linkages testify to a definite and possibly increasing tendency to some vertical disintegration of functions among the leading producers in the Scientific City.

The above description based on table 6.1 and figure 6.4 provides a crude first approximation to the industrial geography of the Scientific City and its adjacent area. In what now follows, a more nuanced account is provided by means of an enquiry into the development of two important sectors in the Scientific City, that is, the electronics industry and the biotechnology industry. Both of these industries are characterized in particular by a proliferation of flexible small and medium-sized enterprises.

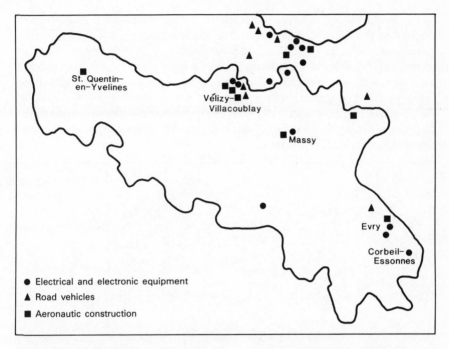

Figure 6.4. Manufacturing establishments employing more than 1000 workers. Source of data: unpublished information in the "Fichier Sirène" Institut National de la Statistique et des Etudes Economiques, Paris, updated by reference to *Kompass Régional Ile de France, 1987*.

The electronics industry

According to unpublished statistics provided by the Groupement des ASSEDIC de la Région Parisienne, there was in 1981 a total of 571 electronics manufacturing establishments in the entire study area (that is, the Scientific City plus that part of the *première couronne* lying between the City and the southern boundary of Paris). The geographical distribution of these establishments is depicted in figure 6.5. Two salient points emerge. First, a dense concentration of relatively large electronics manufacturing establishments lies adjacent to the southern rim of the city of Paris. This concentration is, in fact, part of a (declining) belt of electronics manufacturing activity that coincides more or less irregularly with the whole of the inner suburban ring of Paris. Second, in the Scientific City proper, three incipient nucleations of electronics producers are evident: in and around the two new towns, and in the core area represented above all by the communes of Orsay, Les Ulis, Massy, and Palaiseau. Despite these localized concentrations, there seems to be a remarkably diffuse geographical spread of electronics establishments in the study area, at any rate when compared with the tight agglomerations of producers frequently observable in certain high-technology growth regions of the United States, such as Silicon Valley (see next chapter). This judgment is confirmed by the measured entropy of the spatial pattern of electronics establishments in the Scientific City, where entropy is defined by the expression $-\sum \pi_i \ln \pi_i$, and π_i is the proportion of establishments (relative to all establishments in the Scientific City) in the ith commune. If we express this measure as a percentage of maximum possible entropy [given as $-\ln(1/n)$, with n defined as the total number of communes], we obtain in the present instance a value of 81.6%. This value unambiguously points to the dispersion of the realized locations of electronics manufacturing establishments in the Scientific City proper.

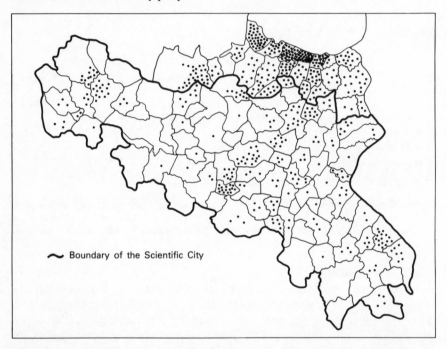

Figure 6.5. Electronics establishments, 1985. Each dot represents one establishment; locations are approximate only. Based on unpublished data provided by Groupement des ASSEDIC de la Région Parisienne.

Although the geography of electronics production over much of the area is, according to the entropy measure, rather amorphous, it is actually highly differentiated relative to more specific criteria. Consider figure 6.6 in which changes in electronics employment between 1975 and 1985 are mapped out. Two distinctive spatial zones are evident, namely, a zone of employment loss coinciding with the inner suburbs, and a zone of employment growth coinciding with the Scientific City proper. Most of the observed losses in the inner suburban zone can be ascribed to plant closures and employment cutbacks as a result of the shift of unskilled assembly work to low-wage areas in the provinces or overseas (IAURIF, 1984).

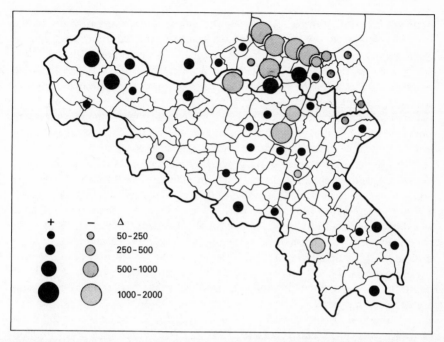

Figure 6.6. Changes in electronics employment by commune, 1975–1985. Based on unpublished data provided by Groupement des ASSEDIC de la Région Parisienne.

Table 6.2 provides further details of these changes. Taken as a whole, the study area lost 3.9% of its employees in the electronics industry between 1975 and 1985. This statistic comprises two main elements: first, a loss of 10.9% in the inner suburban area and, second, a gain of 8.5% in the Scientific City proper. Note that the core area of the Scientific City lost

Table 6.2. Electronics establishments and employment, 1975–1985. Source: Calculated from unpublished data provided by the Groupement des ASSEDIC de la Région Parisienne.

	Employment		Change (%)	Establishments		Change (%)
	1975	1985		1975	1985	
Total study area	46882	45058	− 3.9	319	571	79.0
Southern inner suburbs	29996	26730	− 10.9	207	260	25.6
Scientific City	16886	18328	8.5	112	311	177.7
Core area	3683	2802	− 23.9	20	63	215.0
Rest of Scientific City	13203	15526	17.6	92	248	169.6

employment—at a rate of 23.9% for the whole decade—as a result of the restructuring of a few large establishments in the commune of Massy. Significantly, however, the number of electronics *establishments* in the whole study area increased by 79.0% over the same period, ranging from an increase of 25.6% in the inner suburban zone to an increase of 215.0% in the core area of the City (see table 6.2). Growth in the number of establishments has therefore far outstripped growth of employment, suggesting that a process of rapid small-firm formation and innovation characteristic of emerging flexible industrial complexes has been in operation.

The latter interpretation is reinforced by the data presented in table 6.3. As shown in this table, the average size of electronics establishments in the study area fell dramatically from 147.0 to 79.9 between 1975 and 1985. Furthermore, over the same period of time, a remarkable change in establishment size by geographical locale also occurred. In 1975, average establishment size was smallest in the inner suburban zone and largest in the core area of the Scientific City, with the rest of the City somewhere between these extremes. This locational pattern is characteristic of cases where large capital-intensive branch plants with few external connections are decentralizing to the suburbs. By 1985, after a decade of restructuring and new firm formation in the electronics sector of the Scientific City, the relationship was precisely reversed; now the core area had the smallest establishments on average, and the inner suburbs the largest (table 6.3). In addition, by 1985, the core area had 20.3% of all the electronics establishments in the Scientific City compared with 17.9% in 1975.

The core area has thus begun to emerge definitely, if modestly, as an important focus of new small firm formation and agglomeration in the electronics sector. With its strong concentration of public and private research laboratories and educational institutions, it would seem to be poised on the threshold of a major developmental thrust, and this is now being further encouraged by the implantation of planned industrial parks in the area.

Table 6.3. Average size of electronics edstablishments, 1975 and 1985. Source: Calculated from unpublished data provided by the Groupement des ASSEDIC de la Région Parisienne.

	1975	1985
Total study area	147.0	79.9
Southern inner suburbs	114.9	102.8
Scientific City	145.6	58.9
Core area	184.2	44.5
Rest of Scientific City	143.5	62.5

The biotechnology industry

One of the most rapidly growing sectors in the Scientific City today is the biotechnology industry. This is not so much a homogeneous sector as it is a disparate assemblage of industrial activities whose sole common denominator is a broad but diffuse connection to biological science. In the Scientific City, the industry is engaged in the production of such outputs as antibiotics, blood products, genetic research services, human and animal nutrients, pesticides, pollution controls, and so on; a large segment of the industry is also linked to the growing agro-alimentary production activities of the Scientific City. Establishments in the biotechnology sector tend to be small, highly innovative, and unstable, and to fit into tight and rapidly changing market niches. They also depend heavily on skilled scientific and technical workers.

The locational distribution of manufacturing establishments and private research laboratories in the biotechnology industry in the study area is given by figure 6.7. The figure was drafted on the basis of an address list of members of the Association pour le Développement de la Bio-Industrie; this is a national association and thus figure 6.7 certainly does not represent a

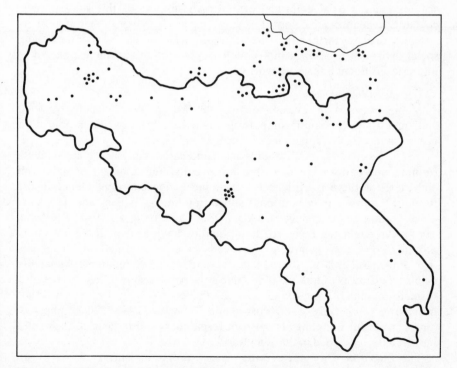

Figure 6.7. Biotechnology manufacturing establishments and private laboratories. Source of data: *Annuaire des Biotechnologies et des Bioindustries*.

complete inventory of biotechnology establishments in the area just as it also surely underrepresents smaller production units. Despite these defects, figure 6.7 provides some useful information. As might be expected, the inner suburban area shows a relatively dense though scattered pattern of plants; this pattern (as in the case of the electronics industry) is again a segment of a heterogeneous zone of production units that surrounds the city of Paris. More interesting for present purposes are two emerging clusters of biotechnology producers in the Scientific City proper. One of these clusters coincides with the new town of St Quentin-en-Yvelines and its surrounding area in the west of the Scientific City. The other is concentrated in and around the high-technology industrial park of Courtaboeuf in the commune of les Ulis in the core area of the City. Establishments in the latter cluster represent especially advanced forms of research and manufacturing in such domains as antibiotics, microbiological products, radioisotopes, sophisticated biotechnology instrumentation systems, and so on.

The biotechnology industry (or at least parts of it) in the Scientific City thus appears to be in the incipient phases of spatial nucleation and differentiation. It is probable that these tendencies are based on increasing interunit linkage and the formation of specialized local labor markets, though only scattered and partial empirical evidence in support of this suggestion is currently available (see below). It seems reasonable to expect that, if markets continue to grow, further agglomeration will occur on the basis of deepening social divisions of labor in biotechnology production and the expansion of interestablishment linkage networks.

An emerging industrial technopole?

The above discussion reveals that over the last couple of decades a varied and quantitatively significant pattern of high-technology industrialization has made its decisive appearance in the Scientific City.

Three recent empirical studies have indicated that the establishments forming this pattern are now starting to constitute a *system* of industrial activities, for there is evidence of their increasing interdependence in the form of input–output relations, subcontracting activities, and technical collaboration and exchange (CSAU, 1986; Davoine et al, 1985; Peyrache, 1984). As might be expected, these studies have shown that local interlinkage of producers is more pronounced in the case of small establishments than in the case of large, for the latter tend to be embedded in more spatially extensive patterns of linkage. The same studies have shown that there is also a small amount of spin-off of new enterprises from local research establishments. Conversely, as Decoster and Tabariés (1986) have indicated, direct and recurrent contacts between researchers and industrialists are still only weakly developed in the Scientific City.

The Scientific City, then, evidently represents an emerging but by no means as yet fully emergent industrial technopole. It is undoubtedly rich in many kinds of agglomeration economies, and it is becoming steadily more so with the passage of time. The City comprises a new industrial space of major dimensions in terms of infrastructure, population, and employment, but has by all appearances not yet quite taken off into a sustained dynamic of accelerated industrialization and system integration such as is observable in parts of the Third Italy. This remark is driven home by the somewhat shapeless character of the industrial geography of much of the Scientific City. In many other high-technology growth regions the clustering and geographical specialization of producers on the basis of their mutual interdependence are much more marked. Even so, the potential for further development of the Scientific City is being actively promoted by the implementation of a series of important policy initiatives whose objective, in effect, is to accelerate the condensation of those precise agglomeration economies needed to propel the region into a virtuous spiral of growth.

The private – public interface in the Scientific City
One of the typical features of French regional development in general and of the growth of the Scientific City in particular is the pervasive presence of the hand of the state. This presence involves both a broad overall framework of regional policy and a series of specific interventions in particular areas. We have already seen how much of the growth of educational and research institutions in the area has been part of a deliberate plan. A series of additional important initiatives in the Scientific City has been focused on the tasks of mobilizing latent agglomeration economies, for there has been an implicit public recognition that development may still be truncated even where all the ingredients of high-technology industrial growth, such as educational institutions, research laboratories, and innovative firms, are assembled in juxtaposition to one another. Before a growth complex in the full sense can emerge, these ingredients must also be brought into functional (flexible) interrelationship via processes of mutual interpenetration, adjustment, and activation. This kind of synergy is by no means necessarily self-engendering. Here, I shall describe two particularly interesting and important cases of collective intervention in the Scientific City representing efforts to enhance its overall industrial performance.

In the first place, the Scientific City Association itself constitutes an attempt to construct a broad organizational framework of development. The basic mission of the Association is to provide the area with a collective identity and to facilitate contacts and information exchanges between the main participants in the development process, that is, local planning agencies, educational institutions, research laboratories, and private firms. It has pursued this second objective in a general and vigorous way. The Association is now engaged in expanding its range of activities and it will shortly enter into partnership with a major financial organization to make available venture capital services for local entrepreneurs. This initiative provides a means of circumventing the rather conservative attitudes and practices of the established French banking system. In this connection, it may be noted that an existing important source of seed money for innovative enterprises is the government-funded Agence Nationale de la Valorisation de la Recherche, with a delegation serving the specific needs of the Ile de France region.

In the second place, the French government has inaugurated a program for the establishment of regional centers for technology innovation and exchange known as CRITTs (*Centre Régionaux d'Innovation et de Transfert de Technologie*). The program was established in 1982 in preparation for the Ninth Plan (1984–88) which lays great stress on the development of new technological poles and on their consolidation by means of planned consultative structures (OECD, 1986; Savy, 1986). Each CRITT is supervised by a regional delegation, itself dependent on the Ministry of Research and Technology. The Ile de France as a whole currently has four different CRITTs (one each for the agro-alimentary, biomedical, integrated circuits, and mechanical engineering industries), and two more (for the biotechnology and instruments industries) are in preparation (cf Danon, 1986). These CRITTs serve the Ile de France region in its entirety, but they nevertheless all have an especially close association with the Scientific City, and three of the four currently in operation are actually located in the City.

Each CRITT seeks to help small innovative firms in its specified domain by bringing researchers and entrepreneurs together and by providing the latter with free technical information and advice. It is no doubt still too early to attempt to evaluate the CRITT program since it is only in its initial phases of development. In principle, however, the CRITTs constitute a potentially significant element in the formation of new technopoles, and no matter whether they eventually prove in their current form to be a success or a failure, they are likely to represent important object lessons for policymakers in other countries. In particular, they would seem to constitute important bridging mechanisms, securing and consolidating agglomeration economies, much like the various umbrella organizations that have come spontaneously into being in the burgeoning industrial districts of the Third Italy. The CRITTs have already gone some way in helping to break down the traditional barriers in France between pure scientific research and industry; and they address directly the circumstance that small-firm innovation is often less a matter of pursuing relentlessly an aprioristic research program than it is, as already suggested, a series of relational practices involving incremental problem-solving in a context of continual mutual readjustment between firms. This relational sense of innovation fits in well with the broad structural concept of agglomeration and polarization sketched out above. It is evident that the Scientific City has still not fully realized its maximum potential in this regard, but the City is also in many ways a sleeping giant, at the threshold of a major developmental surge taking it forward into an endogenous dynamic of organizational fragmentation and intensifying agglomeration.

Conclusion

In this chapter, I have sought to lay out an empirical sketch of the basic geographical anatomy of the Scientific City. I have described the City as a many sided congeries of industrial and social activities, all of which participate interdependently in the territorial reproduction of the whole system. Like many other high-technology industrial complexes in both North America and Western Europe, this system has taken root in a geographical area which (notwithstanding its adjacency to an older industrial zone) has had relatively little previous direct experience of large-scale industrialization and urbanization. It represents not just a new spatial focus of development, but also a new kind of sociopolitical construction as expressed in forms of human settlement and workaday life that differ in important respects from those that were characteristic of earlier rounds of French industrial growth. For one thing, the industries of the Scientific City employ disproportionately large numbers of highly qualified scientific and technical workers (who tend to live in and around its scenic core area). For another, its working-class denizens (a large proportion of them housed in the two new towns) do not constitute quite so refractory a labor force as those generations of workers whose consciousness was forged in the daily experience of life in the great centers of mass production. To be sure, there are several left-wing communes in the area of the Scientific City, mainly along its older northern boundary area, though these have gone out of their way to accommodate new industry, as the communist municipalities of the Third Italy have done. Finally, the industrialization of the Scientific City has taken place in what is for the most part a low-density, semirural area with a rich complement of environmental amenities. It thus provides all of its inhabitants with a congenial atmosphere for domestic life, child rearing, and leisure time activities, which in turn helps (or at least does not hinder) the consolidation of norms of orderly social existence through the entire area.

The structures of work and social reproduction that are currently being set in place in the Scientific City certainly appear to be broadly consonant with smooth industrial expansion. As the regime of flexible accumulation proceeds on its course, the economy of the region will no doubt, for a time at least, continue to develop on the basis of much new entrepreneurial activity and increasing diversification of local labor markets. But from the analysis laid out above, we see that the market alone cannot be relied upon spontaneously and immediately to provide all the necessary coordination to make the industrial system operate at its most efficient level of performance. On the contrary, decisive policy measures have been necessary in the Scientific City, and will assuredly continue to be necessary in order to deal with significant deficiencies of market mechanisms. The wider lesson of all this, no doubt, is that industrial sectors, agglomerations, and regions in the regime of flexible accumulation—for all their dependence on revitalized market structures—remain strongly susceptible to meliorative action in the form of public policy and planning intervention.

The development of the US semiconductor industry and the rise of the Silicon Valley production complex

The semiconductor industry produces outputs that are one of the main foundations of the push to flexibility throughout the economy at large. It is also, in its own right, a modern flexible production sector par excellence. To be sure, there are segments of the industry (for example, discrete device production, microelectronic memories, and some assembly functions) that have evolved significantly in the direction of standardized mass production. Other segments, however (for example, small-batch custom and semicustom producers together with a host of ancillary services), are, if anything, becoming increasingly flexible in their technological and organizational characteristics, and they now constitute one of the most dynamic elements of the industry in the USA today.

The first commercial stirrings of the semiconductor industry date only from the mid-1950s, and its main growth has occurred principally over the last ten to fifteen years. In geographical terms, the industry is typified by a locational structure that can be identified schematically at two distinctive levels. First, at the global level, the industry forms a bipartite pattern of onshore and offshore activities, the former comprising for the most part technologically contrived manufacturing processes (primarily wafer fabrication), the latter encompassing less advanced kinds of production (primarily chip assembly). Second, at the national level, an equally bipartite division can be discerned between a set of Silicon-Valley producers and a set of non-Silicon-Valley producers, with the former exhibiting a comparatively greater tendency to flexibility as manifest in deep social divisions of labor and locational agglomeration.

In the present chapter, I propose to carry out a statistical analysis of the spatial structure of semiconductor manufacturing establishments at this second (that is, national) level of geographical resolution. I shall consider, in particular, the main organizational-*cum*-locational features that differentiate Silicon Valley semiconductor producers from other onshore producers, and that have made Silicon Valley today one of the most dynamic and important high-technology growth centers in the world. I begin by recapitulating some simple information on the semiconductor production process and the current structure of the industry. This information constitutes a necessary prelude to any meaningful locational analysis. I then move forward on this basis into a detailed discussion of the spatial evolution of the onshore industry and of the growth of Silicon Valley.

The US semiconductor industry: production processes and current structure
Semiconductor devices can be broadly classified into two main categories comprising, (a) simple discrete components such as diodes and transistors, and (b) more complicated monolithic integrated circuits (cf Braun and

MacDonald, 1982). The basic technology of discrete semiconductors was developed in the late 1940s, and commercial production was begun in the early 1950s. Integrated circuits were developed in the late 1950s and were successfully manufactured after the discovery of the planar process (that is, multiple fabrication on wafers) by Fairchild Semiconductor Inc. in 1958. Discrete devices and integrated circuits are both produced on a large scale at the present time, but the latter have come to dominate domestic and international semiconductor markets. Much of the early development of semiconductors was linked to military and space procurement programs. However, civilian consumers are nowadays the largest direct and indirect end-users of semiconductor devices. That said, the semiconductor industry continues to be highly dependent on government contracts, especially those parts of it that are engaged in producing leading-edge devices.

Four main stages in the semiconductor manufacturing process may be identified as follows: (a) circuit design and maskmaking, (b) wafer fabrication, (c) assembly, (d) testing. The circuit-design stage involves the resolution of a multitude of technical problems with regard to the particular functions to be performed, the product technology to be used, and the arrangement of the internal architecture of the semiconductor. Once the basic design of the circuit is completed, several photolithographic masks are produced for use in the fabrication process. Fabrication involves the diffusion of chemical impurities into a silicon wafer according to the pattern defined by each mask. This diffusion process is repeated several times as the device is built up layer by layer to the required specifications. Hundreds of devices may be fabricated on a single wafer. The wafers are subsequently cut up into individual components for assembly, packaging, and final test, each of which is an important and complex labor process in its own right.

Every step in the manufacturing process must be carried out according to very precise specifications under carefully controlled environmental conditions. Yield rates for new, complex products may be as low as 10% and below, and a large engineering and technical staff is needed to identify the sources of device failure and to keep the fabrication lines running efficiently. Device assembly is a largely unskilled task, but it, too, must be performed with precision and constantly monitored for failure.

Since its inception, the semiconductor industry has been characterized by a rapid rate of change both in process and in product technologies. Two general patterns of technological development may be particularly noted. First, ever-increasing miniaturization of devices has occurred. Second, every stage of production from circuit design to final test has been increasingly automated as a consequence of intense price competition in high-volume markets. Note, however, that the most advanced and expensive capital equipment is usually employed only by the largest firms producing state-of-the-art devices. Many manufacturers of discrete semiconductors and specialized devices for small market niches continue to use older, less expensive production equipment. These developments have at once facilitated and been driven by incessant innovation and competition. Some sense of the pace of innovation is gleaned from the fact that Hewlett–Packard Inc. derived approximately 50% of its total income in 1984 from products that were no older than three years. Two major conditions of prosperity in the semiconductor industry are an ability to produce larger and larger quantities of devices at lower and lower prices, and/or to identify and develop new products (in particular, custom and semicustom devices) for new markets.

The current structure of the US semiconductor industry reflects this dual pressure to reduce the cost of existing devices and to sustain high rates of new product development. It is marked by both an insistent search for internal economies of scale via enlarged high-volume production units, and a countervailing tendency for some segments to fragment into small units capable of efficiently and flexibly serving specialized niche markets. In addition, the US industry is peculiar (compared with the European and Japanese semiconductor industries) in that it is dominated by independent merchant producers. In Europe and Japan, by contrast, most semiconductor manufacture takes place in large vertically integrated electronics companies. Nevertheless, the number of semiconductor producers captive to vertically integrated electronics companies in the USA (such as Hewlett–Packard Inc. or IBM Inc.) has been increasing in recent years as end-users integrate backwards into semiconductor production and as semiconductor firms integrate forwards into the manufacture of electronic systems products. Captive producers, indeed, now account for some 30% of total US semiconductor output.

As the US semiconductor industry has grown over the last couple of decades, so increasing numbers of subcontractors and suppliers of specialized materials and services have also made their appearance. For example, numerous independent circuit-design houses and specialized fabrication facilities (known as 'silicon foundries') now offer semiconductor manufacturers flexible subcontracting options. At the same time, independent assembly, test, and burn-in subcontractors have started to enter the industry. It will be shown below that the emergence of these specialized service functions has important locational implications for the industry as a whole.

The growth and spread of the US semiconductor industry
The pattern of growth
I begin by tracing out the growth of the semiconductor industry as revealed by statistics for SIC 3674 (semiconductors and related devices) taken from the US *Census of Manufactures* for various years. Note that semiconductors were not recorded as a distinct category in the *Census of Manufactures* until 1963 and, as a result, there is little statistical information on the industry during its incipient phases in the 1950s. However, the *Census of Manufactures* for 1963 does contain some limited tabulations for the semiconductor industry in 1958. Table 7.1 shows total domestic employment and the number of

establishments in SIC 3674 for census years over the period from 1958 to 1982. These data reveal a trend of broad overall growth punctuated only by brief and short-lived period of recession.

Table 7.1. Employment and number of establishments in SIC 3674 (semiconductors and related devices), 1958 – 1982. Source: *Census of Manufactures*.

Year	1958	1963	1967	1972	1977	1982
Total employment (thousands)	23.4	56.3	85.4	97.6	114.0	166.5
Number of establishments	48	107	117	325	545	766

Table 7.2 expands upon the data shown in table 7.1. Here we have information by both census division and state on the geographical distribution of employment in SIC 3674 for the period from 1958 to 1982, though note that the information given for 1958 – 1963 is not strictly comparable with that for 1967 – 1982 as the two sets of data are based on

Table 7.2. Percentage distribution of employment in SIC 3674 (semiconductors and related devices) for census divisions and selected states, 1958 – 1982.

	1958	1963	1967	1972	1977	1982
USA total	100	100	100	100	100	100
New England	29.1	18.0	na	10.7*	10.6	na
Massachusetts	na	11.2	9.4	4.8	4.4	4.4
Mid-Atlantic	34.5	34.3	30.8	21.8	21.7	16.4
New Jersey	na	6.5	6.2	3.5	2.3	1.9
New York	na	8.1	8.5	5.3	10.6	9.0
Pennsylvania	na	19.6	16.1	13.0	8.8	5.5
East N Central	na	na	3.1	9.2	2.3	1.9
West N Central	na	na	0.5	0.8	0.7	na
South Atlantic	na	na	3.5	2.1	2.9	na
Florida	na	na	3.4	1.4	2.6	3.2
East S Central	na	na	na	0.2	na	na
West S Central	na	na	3.1	na	14.5	na
Texas	na	na	3.1	18.3	14.5	13.3
Mountain	na	na	6.3	na	na	na
Arizona	na	9.3	6.3	5.8	14.5	10.7
Pacific	na	na	17.5	na	na	na
California	15.9	19.9	17.5	21.0	27.6	28.7

Source: All data for the years 1958 and 1963 taken from *Census of Manufactures*. All data for the years 1967, 1972, 1977, and 1982 *County Business Patterns* (except where marked by an asterisk which indicates that the source is the *Census of Manufactures*).
na—not available.

different sources. These data show that in the late 1950s the center of the
US semiconductor industry lay not in Silicon Valley but in the Northeast of
the country. In 1958 approximately 63.6% of all employment in the industry
was located in New England and the Mid-Atlantic states of New Jersey, New
York, and Pennsylvania. California contained only some 15.9% of US
semiconductor employment at this time. By the early 1960s, however,
California was beginning to emerge as a major center of semiconductor
production. Thus, as shown in table 7.2, the percentage of employment
located in California increased from 19.9% in 1963 to 21.0% in 1972, and
28.7% in 1982. Much of this employment in California (especially in more
recent years) has been concentrated in Silicon Valley. In 1964 the
proportion of California's total semiconductor employment located in
Silicon Valley was 38.7%, and by 1984 this had risen to 69.2%. Figure 7.1
shows in detail the dramatic growth of the industry in Silicon Valley and its
relative decline in the Northeast. In recent years some significant expansion
of the industry has occurred in other parts of the United States, but Silicon
Valley remains overwhelmingly the dominant spatial focus of the industry.
These shifts in the geography of semiconductor production in the United
States are just one aspect of a more general process of technological and
organizational change.

Recall that in the 1950s the commercial production of semiconductors
was limited to relatively simple discrete devices. Many of the manufacturers
of these devices (such as RCA Inc., Sylvania Inc., and Western Electric Inc.)
were located in the Northeast of the country, where they had already
developed significant facilities for manufacturing vacuum tubes. In the

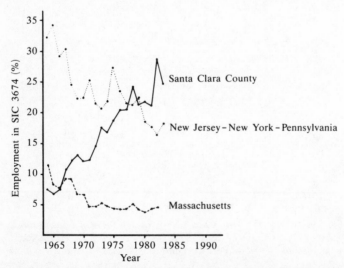

Figure 7.1. Distribution of employment in SIC 3674 (semiconductors and related
devices), 1964 – 1983. Source of data: *County Business Patterns.*

1950s these firms were able successfully to make the transition in situ from vacuum tube production to discrete device production, and in this manner the Northeast developed as the early focus of the semiconductor industry. However, the Northeast was not necessarily the only or even the best possible location for semiconductor production at this time. Among other things, wages were relatively high in the area, and there was a significant union presence in the electrical and electronics industries. From the very first, certain semiconductor manufacturers chose to locate outside of the Northeast. For example, the Motorola Inc. electronics facility which had been established in Phoenix in 1949 rapidly became a major producer of semiconductors; so too did Texas Instruments Inc. which began semiconductor manufacture in Dallas in 1952; and Shockley Laboratories Inc. opened in Santa Clara County in 1955. It may be suggested that, for a brief period in the 1950s, semiconductor production could probably have been carried out profitably at a wide range of locations within the United States. This was especially true of the early leading-edge manufacturers of discrete devices and above all, later in the 1950s, of firms involved in the development of the new and extremely complex integrated circuit technology. The technologies and labor processes of integrated circuit production were so novel that these firms were obliged at the time to produce internally much of their own materials, machinery, and equipment, as well as their own specialized technical services and know-how (Glasmeier, 1985). As a result, advanced semiconductor manufacturers during the 1950s were in all probability only weakly attracted to the linkage and local labor-market opportunities of preexisting industrial electronics complexes. Rather, a window of locational opportunity (as described in chapter 2) seemed to have opened and, for a time at least, it was possible for these firms to operate successfully at many different locations in the United States.

During the late-1950s and 1960s a number of these leading-edge semiconductor manufacturers chose to locate in what was to become Silicon Valley. Shockley Laboratories had located there in 1955, and Fairchild Semiconductor, National Semiconductor, and Rheem Inc. followed in short order. Data from *County Business Patterns* reveal that semiconductor employment in the region increased slowly at first to a total of 4164 in just eight establishments in 1965. We may note that the semiconductor industry in Silicon Valley at this date was only slightly larger (in terms of total employment) than it was in Phoenix or Dallas. However, over the course of the next few years, the industry began to grow much faster in Silicon Valley than at any other location in the United States. Just why Silicon Valley developed at this time into the privileged hub of the semiconductor industry (above all for integrated circuit production) remains far from clear; this problem is broached again in the following section. It does appear evident, however, that, once the process of growth had begun, the region acquired a very significant and potent stock of agglomeration economies that reinforced its increasing locational dominance. It soon began to draw into its spatial orbit specialized service and input industries, and it also developed a burgeoning specialized labor-market for semiconductor engineers and other technical personnel. By the end of the 1960s, after a decade of prolific horizontal disintegration, or spin-off, there were twenty-six semiconductor establishments in Silicon Valley employing more than 12 000 workers.

Neither Motorola in Phoenix, nor Texas Instruments in Dallas, generated such a series of local spin-off ventures. Nor did the specialized disintegrated input suppliers or ancillary subcontractors, so characteristic of Silicon Valley, appear in a major way in Phoenix or Dallas. At the same time, most of the vertically-integrated electronics firms manufacturing discrete semi-conductor devices in the Northeast failed signally to make an effective transition into the production of integrated circuits, and these firms gradually fell out of the ranks of the leading semiconductor companies. The industry in the Northeast as a whole has remained largely devoted to the production of discrete semiconductor devices only (see table 7.3). Silicon Valley, by contrast, expanded at a particularly fast pace during the late 1960s and early 1970s, and the region soon became the major focus of advanced production and technological innovation in the entire industry. At the present time Silicon Valley accounts for almost 25% of the total US semiconductor work force.

Table 7.3. Shipments of discrete semiconductor devices and integrated circuits in 1982 for selected states. Source: *Census of Manufactures*, 1982.

	Discrete devices (transistors, diodes and rectifiers) (%)	Integrated circuits (%)
Arizona	na	6.3
California	21.8	33.3
Florida	na	3.1
Massachusetts	12.5	2.4
New Jersey	2.4	1.0
New York	1.9	na
Pennsylvania	12.5	na
Texas	na	16.2
Total US shipments ($ millions)	1102.3	7298.4

na—not available.

Despite this remarkable and indeed intensifying geographical concentration of the semiconductor industry in Silicon Valley, from the very beginning a complementary process of locational dispersal been going on simultaneously. This trend is captured in figure 7.2 which shows the percentage of US states with at least one semiconductor manufacturing establishment for each year over the period from 1964 to 1982. A logistic curve has been superimposed over the data points shown in figure 7.2 and extrapolated backwards and forwards. If the trend represented by this curve continues, we may expect that, by the year 2000, over 95% of all US states will have at least one semiconductor establishment. Most of these more dispersed establishments seem to be either (a) discrete device producers, (b) branch fabrication facilities engaged in the mass production of high-volume products (such as computer-memory devices), or (c) captive plants.

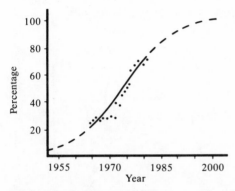

Figure 7.2. Percentage of US states with at least one semiconductor establishment, 1964–1982. Source of data: *County Business Patterns*.

The contemporary geography of the semiconductor industry in the United States
In order to supplement the statistical information available from published sources, an effort was made to compile a list of addresses of all semiconductor establishments currently operating onshore in the United States. The list was assembled in mid-1985 on the basis of information taken from industrial directories, commercial data files, company reports, and direct contacts with semiconductor industry representatives.

The semiconductor manufacturers included in this list differ in two important respects from the official definition of the industry as codified in SIC 3674 (semiconductors and related devices). First, the official definition of SIC 3674 allows for the inclusion of subcontractors, consultants, and suppliers who are allied to the industry but do not themselves manufacture semiconductor devices; such ancillary activities have been excluded from the data set established here. Second, manufacturers of hybrid and film circuits have also been excluded on the grounds that certain of the labor processes involved in the production of these devices are quite different from those employed in the production of discrete semiconductors and monolithic integrated circuits. The address list on which the following analyses are based refers uniquely to manufacturers of the latter two categories of devices.

The data set identifies the locations of 590 semiconductor establishments in total, and this tally is thought to be virtually complete. It may be

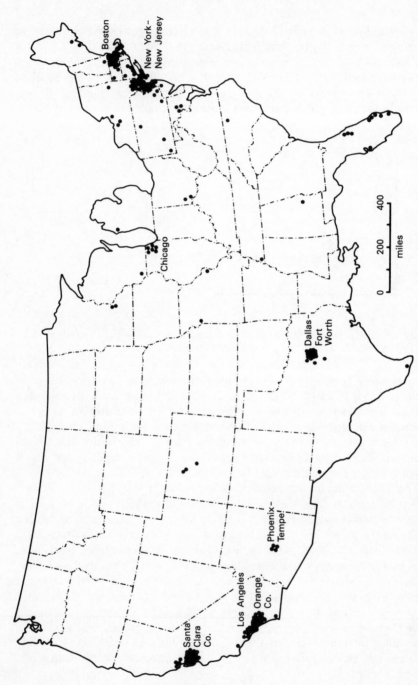

Figure 7.3. Geographical distribution of discrete device manufacturing establishments in the United States.

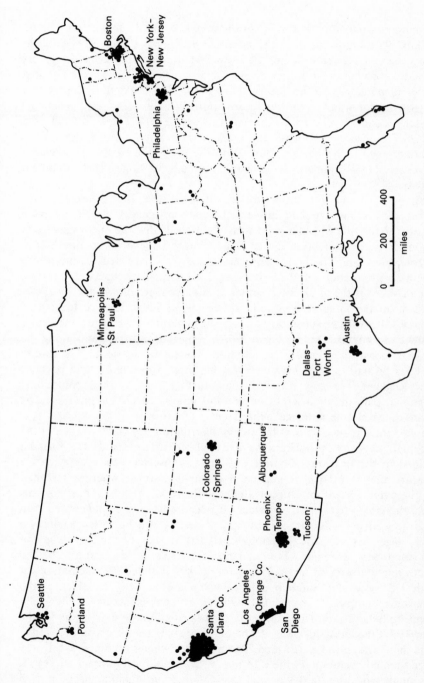

Figure 7.4. Geographical distribution of integrated circuit manufacturing establishments in the United States.

compared with data from *County Business Patterns* for 1985 which reports a total of 791 establishments classified under SIC 3674. Of the 590 establishments under investigation here, 227 (38.5%) are discrete device producers (including producers of optoelectronic devices), 290 (49.2%) are integrated circuit manufacturers, and the remaining 73 (12.4%) cannot be precisely categorized for want of further information. Whereas most establishments produce uniquely one or the other kind of device type, some do produce a mixture of discrete devices and integrated circuits, though the one is invariably subsidiary to the other. With the exception of the 73 unclassifiable cases, establishments have been grouped according to their dominant activity.

Figures 7.3 and 7.4 show the locations of the 227 discrete device manufacturers and the 290 integrated circuit producers that it has been possible to identify by category. Figure 7.3 reveals that the major centers of discrete device production are in Massachusetts, the Mid-Atlantic States, Silicon Valley, and Southern California. Clearly, the Northeast continues to dominate production of these devices. By contrast, as figure 7.4 shows, Silicon Valley is the undisputed center of integrated circuit production. Fully 45% of all the integrated circuit establishments identified are located in Silicon Valley. Other subsidiary clusters of integrated circuit producers are evident in Phoenix, Dallas – Forth Worth, Colorado Springs, and along the Atlantic coast of Florida. In addition, there are scattered fabrication facilities located in New Mexico, Oregon, Utah, Washington, and parts of New England. We may develop some further sense of the contrasting locational patterns of discrete device and integrated circuit producers by means of two simple statistical experiments as follows.

First, entropy measures of the spatial distribution, by state, of each of the two main types of producers were calculated according to the formula defined in the previous chapter. The map of discrete producers yields a measure that is 60.6% of maximum possible entropy, whereas the map of integrated circuit producers yields a figure of 48.1%. Thus, on this criterion, integrated circuit producers are definitely more agglomerated than discrete device producers; this important finding will be raised again at a later stage. Second, the locational patterns of the two major types of semiconductor producers were analyzed relative to the pattern of the electronics industry at large. The exercise was initiated by calculating for each US state the number of establishments in SIC 36 (electric and electronic equipment) minus the number of establishments in SIC 3674 (semiconductors and related devices). This calculation was carried out for the year 1982, the latest year for which complete statistics were available at the time the research was performed. The numerical values obtained in this way were then correlated with the information collected in the direct survey on the number of discrete device and integrated circuit manufacturers in each state. The results of this correlation analysis are given in table 7.4. The correlations were computed first by using data for all US states, and they were then repeated a second time with California excluded from the analysis. Because so much electronics and semiconductor production is concentrated in California, the single bivariate observation for this state dominates to an excessive degree the entire analysis. By excluding California, a clearer sense of the relationship under examination for the rest of the country is obtained. The results indicate that semiconductor producers of all kinds are locationally associated with electrical and electronics industrial complexes in general. However, the correlations are much stronger for discrete semiconductor producers than for integrated circuit producers. This suggests that manufacturers of discrete devices can survive effectively on the basis of very generalized sorts of agglomeration economies, whereas manufacturers of integrated circuits are evidently much more dependent on more highly specialized kinds of agglomeration economies, and these are available only at a relatively restricted set of locations. That is why, no doubt, such a marked contrast can be observed between the locational patterns of the two types of manufacturers, with those specializing in the production of integrated circuits being pre-eminently focused on Silicon Valley.

Table 7.4. Coefficients of correlation between (a) electric and electronics equipment establishments, and (b) number of semiconductor establishments, across states, 1982. (See text for more precise definition.)

	Discrete semiconductor establishments	Integrated circuit establishments
All states	0.923	0.857
All states excluding California	0.791	0.529

The Silicon-Valley complex: some historical and geographical details
Silicon Valley is the organizational and locational nexus of the whole US semiconductor industry. In what follows, I shall provide some substantive historical and geographical details concerning the development of the industry in Silicon Valley from the point of view of the theoretical ideas laid out in chapters 3 and 4. Supplementary empirical information can be obtained from Bernstein et al (1977), Green (1983), Rogers and Larson (1984), and Saxenian (1983). The broad geographical situation of the area is depicted by figure 7.5.

The genesis of Silicon Valley
As already suggested, it is far from clear why the semiconductor industry developed in Silicon Valley in the first place. Most accounts of the process seem to stress what I have pejoratively alluded to earlier (in the introduction to chapter 3) as a series of unique 'locational factors'. Three of these have received particular attention in the literature. First, much has been made of the early role of Stanford University in Palo Alto, which, from the very

beginning, provided a local source of skilled engineering and technical personnel, and presciently laid out one of the first high-technology industrial parks in the United States. Second, several electronics companies (for example, Hewlett–Packard Inc. and Varian Inc.) had already located in Silicon Valley prior to the establishment of the first semiconductor firm in the region by Shockley in 1955; presumably, these electronics firms helped to create some low-level but positive agglomeration economies. Third, the San Francisco Bay Area contained several major military and aerospace installations (such as Moffett Field Naval Air Station in Mountain View) that constituted a strong potential market for electronics devices and helped to create a pool of scientists and engineers in the region. There can be little doubt that these different locational attractions had definite influences on the development of the semiconductor industry in Silicon Valley. However, combinations of equally favorable conditions existed at many other locations in the United States, and there is no especial reason why we should ascribe a markedly superior locational attractiveness to Santa Clara County at this time. It is probable that there were other locations (for instance in Southern California, Arizona, Florida, or Texas) that were as well or even more suited to the peculiar locational needs of the industry in its incipient phases of development.

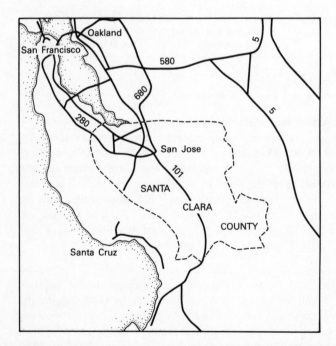

Figure 7.5. Santa Clara County (Silicon Valley) in geographical context; major highways shown by number.

To repeat, it seems likely that, for a brief period in the 1950s, it was feasible to carry out semiconductor production profitably at a wide range of locations in the United States. The kinds of location factors that have been commonly advanced to account for the early growth of the semiconductor industry in Silicon Valley simply did not constitute irresistible advantages, but only a set of adjunct contingencies widely available in varying combinations elsewhere. Nevertheless, by the early 1960s, a process of vertical and horizontal disintegration and local labor-market formation had been initiated among Silicon-Valley semiconductor firms so that many important agglomeration economies started to become available in the region, especially for integrated circuit producers. As this happened, production costs in Silicon Valley presumably fell and, concomitantly, other locational options for the emerging integrated circuit industry became steadily less attractive. A subdued version of this same agglomeration process seems to have affected the locational activity of discrete device producers in the Northeast of the country in the 1950s and 1960s. The reasons why such strongly developed processes of agglomeration appeared at such an early period in Silicon Valley rather than at any of the other nascent centers of integrated circuit production in the United States (in Phoenix and Dallas, above all) are not at all obvious. It may be that the particular corporate structures of Motorola in Phoenix, and Texas Instruments in Dallas discouraged horizontal and/or vertical disintegration (spin-off) and encouraged the internalization of new product and process innovations, whereas Shockley Laboratories and later Fairchild Semiconductors in Silicon Valley, were unable at the outset to achieve the same level of organizational control. Unfortunately, currently available data do not allow a more careful sifting of these issues. Indeed it may be said that the question of the initiation and early consolidation of growth centers in capitalism (from 19th century Lancashire to Henry Ford's Detroit to Silicon Valley) has never really been satisfactorily addressed or resolved. In any event, by the mid-1960s Silicon Valley had become the major hub of the semiconductor industry, and its preeminent position has been progressively reinforced over the 1970s and 1980s.

The pattern of growth in Silicon Valley

Employment in the semiconductor industry in Silicon Valley grew steadily from 3994 in 1964 to 47069 in 1985 (see table 7.5). Over the same time period the number of semiconductor establishments in the Valley grew from 7 to 136. Much of this growth, as noted, has been based on the manufacture of integrated circuits.

The expansion of semiconductor production in the Valley has been accompanied by substantial upstream and downstream industrial development which has helped to underpin the local stock of agglomeration economies. This point is illustrated by the data presented in table 7.6 which shows employment in selected high-technology industrial sectors in Silicon

Valley from 1962 to 1982. All of these sectors are in one way or another associated with the semiconductor industry, either as producers, suppliers of inputs, or as direct and indirect consumers of finished devices. Notice that employment in the core high-technology complex (defined here as SIC categories 35, 36, 37, and 38) grew from 23 774 in 1962 to 228 873 in 1982. The contribution of SIC 3674 to this core of high-technology employment has actually increased slightly from 15.6% in 1967 to 22.3% in 1982. It is of especial interest to observe that employment in SIC 3573 (electronic computing equipment) has expanded from 9657 in 1972 to 55 956 in 1982. Employment in this latter sector in Silicon Valley now in fact exceeds employment in SIC 3674. In a recent survey, Business Directories Inc. (1985) identified a total of more than 2700 establishments involved in high-technology manufacturing activities in Silicon Valley.

The agglomeration economies of Silicon Valley have been further intensified by the development of large populations in local urban communities. These populations are the basis of extensive labor markets in electronics personnel. The overall population of Santa Clara County grew from 642 315 in 1960 to 1 064 714 in 1970 to 1 295 071 in 1980. A large pool of skilled technical and engineering workers has been established in Silicon Valley, and extremely fluid local labor markets seem to have developed around this category of high-wage but very mobile workers. In addition a large proportion of the population is made up of Hispanic and Asian immigrants. These immigrants form a constantly expanding pool of low-wage nonunionized workers. According to the 1980 *Census of Population and Housing*, 17.5% of the population of Santa Clara County is of Hispanic origin, and a further 7.8% is of Asian–Pacific Islander origin. Silicon Valley thus has a highly segmented labor force comprising managerial and technical cadres on the one side and unskilled immigrants

Table 7.5. Employment and number of establishments in SIC 3674 (semiconductors and related devices), Santa Clara County, 1964–1985. Source: *County Business Patterns*.

Year	Total employment	Number of establishments	Year	Total employment	Number of establishments
1964	3 994	7	1975	18 786	53
1965	4 164	8	1976	21 779	63
1966	6 042	9	1977	24 988	65
1967	8 377	8	1978	29 578	67
1968	10 095	8	1979	28 810	91
1969	12 338	15	1980	34 453	92
1970	12 290	26	1981	34 775	108
1971	9 684	28	1982	50 998	135
1972	11 491	35	1983	39 589	127
1973	16 388	36	1984	43 661	134
1974	24 432	49	1985	47 069	136

on the other. On this basis, semiconductor producers have been able to reconstruct the industrial employment relation anew and, for the moment, to ward off any latent tendencies to unionization among their production workers.

Table 7.6. The structure of manufacturing employment in Santa Clara County, 1962 – 1982. Source: *County Business Patterns*.

SIC	Sector	1962	1967	1972	1977	1982
35	Machinery (except electrical)	6 202	14 125	19 779	33 392	69 806
357	Office and computing machines	na	na	10 099	26 231	60 152
3573	Electronic computing equipment	na	na	9 657	na	55 956
36	Electric and electronic equipment	14 120	31 620	42 536	53 557	101 807
362	Electrical industrial apparatus	120	na	625	785	898
366	Communication equipment	2 058	7 109	6 701	11 156	25 710
367	Electronic components and accessories	6 303	6 322	25 101	38 494	71 128
3674	Semiconductors and related devices	na	8 377	11 491	24 988	50 998
37	Transportation equipment	2 811	6 265	5 453	25 278	32 236
376	Guided missiles, space vehicles and parts	na	na	na	17 500[a]	17 500[a]
38	Instruments and related products	641	1 481	2 190	17 893	25 024
382	Measuring and controlling devices	na	na	na	12 694	17 376
383	Optical instruments and lenses	na	na	375	na	1 875
	All other manufacturing	53 126	60 883	54 701	44 878	53 979
	Total employment in manufacturing	76 900	114 374	124 659	174 998	282 852

[a] Median value of the interval 10 000 – 24 999.
na—not available.

The contemporary industrial geography of Silicon Valley

All of these many dimensions of growth have given rise to a large and multifaceted industrial complex in Silicon Valley today. Let us briefly consider in simple empirical terms the main geographical outlines of this complex and its principal internal sources of agglomeration economies.

Figure 7.6 shows the locations of discrete device and integrated circuit producers in Silicon Valley, and is derived from the address list of semiconductor establishments described above. Note that semiconductor producers of both major types are tightly clustered together in the four central communities of Mountain View, San Jose, Santa Clara, and Sunnyvale, where they are closely associated with a variety of upstream suppliers and downstream customers. Two major points now need to be made.

First, semiconductor production in Silicon Valley is supported by a phalanx of specialized input suppliers and subcontractors who constitute one of the important sources of agglomeration economies in the region. Figure 7.7 depicts the geographical distribution of some of the more important of these suppliers and subcontractors, namely, device-assembly houses, circuit-design establishments, maskmakers, independent test facilities, and other ancillary subcontractors. The close locational association between these establishments and semiconductor producers undoubtedly reflects the intricate functional relations that run between them.

Second, as the data presented in table 7.6 indicate, Silicon Valley is also a major locational focus for users of semiconductor devices. The locational

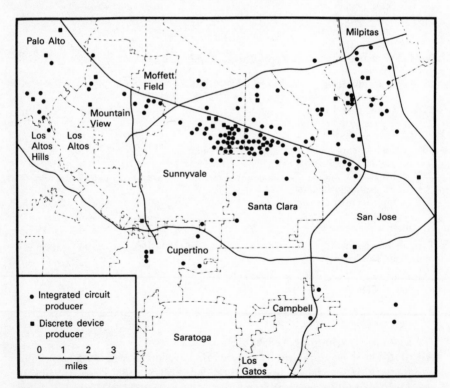

Figure 7.6. Geographical distribution of semiconductor manufacturing establishments in Silicon Valley.

correlation of semiconductor manufacturers with many of their main customers reduces the cost of transactional relations between these two groups of firms. Among the more important customers for semiconductor products are computer manufacturers (for microprocessors and memory circuits form the basic operating units of all modern computers). In figure 7.8 the geographical distribution of computer manufacturing establishments in Silicon Valley is indicated and once more the marked geographical correspondence with the semiconductor industry is apparent.

In these ways, Silicon Valley has evolved, and continues to evolve, as a many sided high-technology complex focused on the semiconductor industry and its associated suppliers and customers. It has been suggested by some analysts (for example, Saxenian, 1983) that the continued growth of Silicon Valley may now be in some doubt, and that the rising incidence of agglomeration diseconomies (such as labor and housing shortages and environmental pollution) is beginning to drive away new investments. These analysts point to the increasing dispersal of fabrication and assembly tasks to various peripheral locations as evidence of this process. The present

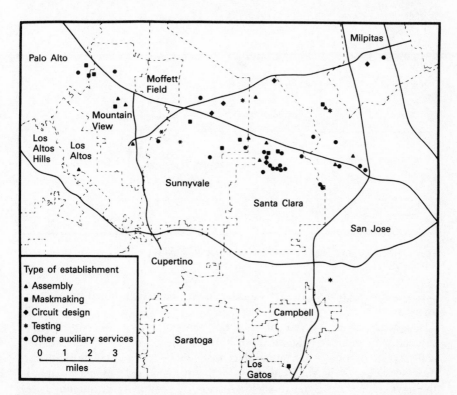

Figure 7.7. Geographical distribution of specialized semiconductor subcontractor establishments in Silicon Valley.

investigation, however, indicates that, while this dispersal has indeed been going on, it is simultaneously associated with the continued expansion of semiconductor employment in Silicon Valley. The Valley remains the primary center of research and advanced production in the US semiconductor industry, and (with the exception of occasional and temporary downturns sparked off by cyclical recessions in the industry, as in 1975, 1981, and the mid-1980s) there is little evidence as yet of a permanent reversal of this state of affairs, even with intensified Japanese competition.

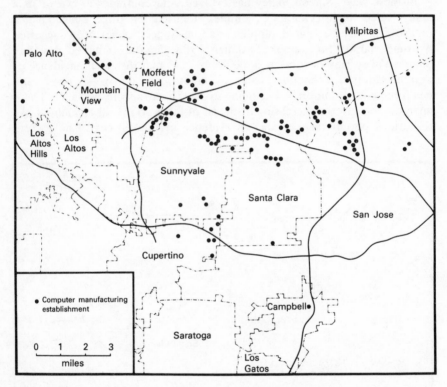

Figure 7.8. Geographical distribution of computer manufacturing establishments in Silicon Valley.

The spatial structure of the US semiconductor industry: a linear discriminant analysis

The geographical pattern of the US semiconductor industry is now subjected to detailed statistical scrutiny by means of linear discriminant analysis. In particular, an attempt is made here to examine the concrete processes underlying the industry's dominant locational tendencies, that is, the development of a dense agglomeration of producers in Silicon Valley, and a relatively loose network of plants throughout the remainder of the country. To be sure, there is some modest agglomeration of semiconductor establishments in places outside of Silicon Valley (for example, in Southern California, the Phoenix area, parts of Colorado, Texas, and the Northeast United States), though none of these places matches the size, density, and diversity of the Silicon-Valley complex. I now test the hypothesis that a bipartite classification of producers (depending upon whether they are located inside or outside of Silicon Valley) can be sustained in ways that are consistent with the account of agglomeration and locational dispersal laid out in earlier sections of this book.

Towards an analysis
The argument here is based upon original data collected in a mail questionnaire survey of all the 590 semiconductor manufacturing establishments identified in the address list described above. Of the total 590 questionnaires sent out, only 60 (10.2%) were eventually returned, and not all of these returns were fully usable as many respondents provided incomplete information. The low response rate to the questionnaire survey can probably be accounted for by the rather proprietary nature of much of the information requested, and the time needed to fill out the questionnaire. Despite this difficulty, the data obtained provide a serviceable basis for further analysis. Table 7.7 shows in cross-tabulated form, according to location and type of production, the percentage distribution of the 60 establishments in the final sample. Corresponding percentages for the total population of semiconductor establishments are also shown. A χ^2 test (with one degree of freedom) reveals there is no significant difference at the 95% confidence level between these two sets of percentages.

The data collected in the questionnaire survey consist of direct measures of plant activity as revealed by various indices of employment, technologies-in-use, outputs, external linkages, ownership status, and so on. All of these measures were derived from the theoretical ideas sketched out at an earlier

Table 7.7. Percentage distribution of semiconductor establishments surveyed, according to location and type.

	Silicon-Valley	Non-Silicon-Valley	Total
Sample (60 establishments)			
Discrete device producers	8.3	28.3	36.6
Integrated circuit producers	31.7	31.7	63.4
Total	40.0	60.0	100.0
Population (517 establishments[a])			
Discrete device producers	5.6	38.3	43.9
Integrated circuit producers	25.3	30.8	56.1
Total	30.9	69.1	100.0

[a] The population consists of the 517 establishments (out of a total of 590) that it has been possible to classify by type.

stage about the locational effects of production processes, transactional activity, and local labor markets. These data were then subjected to discriminant analysis, which is a statistical technique for identifying the differences between two or more pregiven groups of observations on the basis of a set of diagnostic variables. In the present instance, this involves an attempt to separate Silicon-Valley producers from non-Silicon-Valley producers according to various indices of plant activity. Discriminant analysis defines a linear weighted combination of these indices in such a way as maximally to distinguish one group from the other. This discriminant function, as it is called, transforms the values of the original set of variables into a set of discriminant scores. The discriminant scores may then be used to classify producers into one of the two groups, and the proportion of producers correctly classified is a measure of the success of the discriminant function. Standardized discriminant function coefficients are assigned to each of the variables in the discriminant function and these may be used to assay the sense (or otherwise) of the exercise.

Results of the analysis

Three separate linear discriminant analyses were performed for (a) a pooled data set representing all plants in the sample, (b) integrated circuit producers only, and (c) discrete device producers only. The results are summarized in tables 7.8 and 7.9. In each analysis, the same four variables were found consistently to provide the best results in terms of theoretical reasonableness and separation of Silicon-Valley from non-Silicon-Valley producers. I shall first of all simply list the four variables, and then I shall comment on their meaning. Recall that *establishments* (and not firms) are the unit of observation on which this analysis is based. The variables are (a) the percentage of all employees engaged in R&D activities, (b) the average diameter of semiconductor wafers used in the production process, (c) merchant/captive status (this variable is scored 1 if the establishment is merchant, and 0 if it is captive), (d) the percentage of total *merchant* output

Table 7.8. Standardized canonical discriminant function coefficients for Silicon-Valley versus non-Silicon-Valley semiconductor manufacturers.

	All establishments	Integrated circuit producers	Discrete device producers
Percentage of employees in R&D	0.3843**	0.2357**	0.5111*
Diameter of wafers	0.6609**	0.6908**	0.0892
Merchant versus captive producer	0.6061**	0.6337**	0.1655
Percentage of merchant sales in county	0.7496**	0.7538**	0.6819*

* Significant at the 0.05 level. ** Significant at the 0.01 level.

that is sold to other establishments in the same county. These variables provide a useful, though as I shall show, somewhat limited operationalization of the earlier theoretical arguments.

Let us now refer back to these arguments. It was suggested that establishments with flexible transactions-intensive relations with one another will have a certain tendency to cluster together. By contrast, establishments with more limited, more stable, and low-cost external linkages will, on this count, be under less pressure to locate in close proximity to one another. Spatially clustered plants, moreover, will be able to take advantage of the external economies that are engendered by their joint activation of a large local labor market. Among the many such economies, expeditious recruitment of both skilled and unskilled labor must surely be of major importance. Certain types of semiconductor manufacturers might be expected to be especially susceptible to these inducements to agglomeration. Such manufacturers include (a) establishments serving low-volume, custom and semicustom markets, (b) establishments involved in prototype and new product development, and (c) establishments manufacturing low-yield state-of-the-art devices. By contrast, producers using routinized procedures to manufacture more standardized outputs in high volume would be expected to be less dependent upon agglomeration economies. These remarks are based on three main observations. First, producers of low-volume, custom and semicustom products will tend to have relatively problematical external linkages (both input and output) calling for complex intermediation of order specifications, whereas standardized producers will be able to transact larger volumes of business at much lower unit costs. Second, these low-volume, custom and semicustom, as well as prototype, producers consume a variety of specialized services in small quantities at irregular intervals, and such services are usually most efficiently provided by vertically disintegrated independent subcontractors and suppliers. Third, establishments involved in new product development are likely to have variable and unpredictable demands for highly skilled

Table 7.9. Linear discriminant analysis of Silicon-Valley versus non-Silicon-Valley semiconductor manufacturers: summary statistics

	All establishments	Integrated circuit producers	Discrete device producers
Number of establishments analyzed	44	28	16
Percentage of establishments correctly classified	90.91	92.90	81.25
Canonical correlation	0.75**	0.78**	0.58

** Significant at the 0.01 level.

engineering and technical staff, such that employers and employees both find it to their advantage to be located in an area where there is a constantly circulating pool of appropriate job vacancies and qualified applicants. Establishments involved in the mass production of mature devices, by contrast, may be expected to have more stable labor demands. If these latter producers are also able to maintain low rates of labor turnover, they may become relatively independent of external labor markets and, as a result, less dependent on the various agglomeration economies that derive from access to a highly developed regional pool of workers.

If these arguments are correct, it ought to be possible to distinguish Silicon-Valley producers from non-Silicon-Valley producers on the basis of relevant technologies, organization, and associated transactional and employment characteristics. This is what the four variables identified above accomplish in the discriminant analysis (see table 7.8). The meaning of each of these variables is now examined in turn. First, the revealed high percentage of research and development workers employed by Silicon-Valley semiconductor establishments suggests that this region is a hotbed of technological innovation (both in processes and in products) for the industry as a whole. Second, the relatively large diameter of the wafers used by Silicon-Valley producers is direct testimony to their leading-edge status; by the same token, Silicon Valley has comparatively few of the low-technology discrete device manufacturers (who predominantly use 2-inch wafers) that are scattered throughout the rest of the country. Third, the finding that merchant producers are strongly attracted to Silicon Valley whereas captive plants are overwhelmingly located elsewhere is symptomatic of the peculiar external transactional relations of these two types of producers. Merchant producers must maintain widely ranging and problematical linkage relations with a variety of customers, very many of whom are located in Silicon Valley. Captive plants, by contrast, manufacture exclusively for their parent companies and thus face a much more restricted set of linkage relations. Furthermore, captive plants are to some extent sheltered from the direct competition that pervades merchant markets. This means that they can more readily operate at locations lacking the sorts of agglomeration economies available in Silicon Valley; and, indeed, they often tend to be located outside of Silicon Valley and close to the parent plants that they serve. Fourth and last, and in direct corroboration of all the above, we find that Silicon-Valley producers sell a much higher proportion of their merchant output to customers in their immediate vicinity than do establishments in other parts of the country. This indicates that semiconductor production in Silicon Valley is in part sustained by a closely knit web of *intra*regional transactional relations among many different independent but functionally related producers. This result adds further credence to the argument concerning the transactional economies to be derived from locating in the specialized production complex of Silicon Valley.

We can now add to our sense of the problem in hand by comparing the three different linear discriminant analyses laid out in tables 7.8 and 7.9. Quite obviously the results are very successful for the cases of (a) all plants, and (b) integrated circuit producers. The discriminant analysis was much less successful in the case of discrete device producers. I interpret this to be a reflection of the generally lower technological level of discrete device production (as compared with integrated circuit production), and consequently, Silicon Valley is not such a dominant locational reference point for this segment of the industry. Hence, discrimination between Silicon-Valley and non-Silicon-Valley producers cannot be expected to be as meaningful in this case. Instead, as shown, discrete device production seems to be facilitated by generalized agglomeration economies available in electrical and electronics industrial complexes in many different parts of the United States. I should add that the very limited number of degrees of freedom in the case of the analysis of discrete producers has also had a depressive effect on the levels of statistical significance achieved, though the signs of all the coefficients are consistent with the rest of the analysis.

The classificatory power of each of the three analyses is remarkably high. In the analyses of all establishments and integrated circuit producers, over 90% of all plants are correctly classified, and the canonical correlation in each case is very significant. In the case of discrete producers, the number of plants correctly classified is of the order of 81%, but the associated canonical correlation coefficient is nonsignificant, for with only sixteen observations (in a four-variable model) the probability of correct classification some four times out of five on the basis of purely random trials is already quite high.

Extension of the analysis

These discriminant analyses provide a coherent, but limited, account of the characteristics of the semiconductor industry both inside and outside of Silicon Valley. In the questionnaire survey, data were collected on many variables in addition to the four dealt with above. Several of these other variables contain much useful information. However, it was not possible to include them all simultaneously in the discriminant analysis as they are highly correlated both with each other and with the four variables already used. I therefore now pursue another line of attack in order to extract some of the additional information available in this enlarged set of variables.

A basic output of the discriminant analyses described above is a set of discriminant scores. Recall that a discriminant score is the sum of the original values of the input variables weighted by the discriminant function coefficients. It is this measure that prescribes to which classificatory category a given observation will be assigned. In the present instance, the discriminant score is an index of the likely locational definition of any plant, ranging from extremely probable association with Silicon Valley (a high score) to extremely unlikely association (a low score). Correlation coefficients relating these discriminant scores to the additional measures of plant activity were calculated, and the results of this exercise are reported in table 7.10 for (again) all establishments, integrated circuit producers, and discrete device producers. Note that these correlation coefficients differ widely from one another in terms of their degrees of freedom, for much data was missing from the questionnaires that were returned.

Table 7.10. Pearsonian coefficients of correlation between discriminant scores and selected variables for Silicon-Valley versus non-Silicon-Valley semiconductor manufacturers.

Variable[a]	All plants		Integrated circuit producers		Discrete device producers	
	r	*n*	*r*	*n*	*r*	*n*
Plant size (total employment)	− 0.00	44	− 0.17	28	− 0.02	16
Employees, production workers (%)	− 0.20	44	0.10	28	− 0.04	16
Employees, female (%)	− 0.03	44	0.29	28	0.26	16
Employees in R&D (%)	0.36**	44	0.21	28	0.84**	16
Employees in circuit design (%)	0.44**	44	0.34*	27	0.33	15
Average wage of production workers	0.21	40	0.10	25	0.18	15
Output of integrated circuits (%)	0.49**	44	0.40*	28	0.24*	16
Output of discretes (%)	− 0.46**	44	− 0.17	28	0.04	16
Output, application specific (%)	− 0.11	44	− 0.19	28	0.03	16
Age of fabrication	− 0.38**	41	− 0.37*	25	− 0.25	16
Diameter of wafers	0.56**	44	0.57**	28	− 0.36	16
Average plant yield rate	− 0.21	35	− 0.08	19	− 0.41	16
Average feature size	− 0.31*	37	− 0.25	27	− 0.44	10
Merchant/captive producer (binary)	0.48**	44	0.72**	28	0.22	16
Single-establishment firm (binary)	0.17	43	0.29	28	− 0.14	15
Assembly completed on-site (%)	− 0.46**	42	− 0.47**	26	0.04	16
Assembly completed at a branch plant (%)	− 0.06	39	0.06	23	− 0.11	16
Assembly completed by subcontractors (%)	0.54**	39	0.36*	23	0.15	16
Merchant sales in county (%)	0.72**	44	0.65**	28	0.91**	16
Merchant sales in state (%)	0.69	44	0.69**	28	0.64**	16

[a] Italicized variables enter into the discriminant analysis.
* Significant at the 0.05 level. ** Significant at the 0.01 level.

The results displayed in table 7.10 reconfirm strongly the general interpretation of the earlier exercises. In particular, the correlation coefficients forcefully corroborate the assessment of Silicon Valley as a center of research-intensive and engineering-intensive forms of leading-edge semiconductor production and, above all, complex unstandardized device production. Semiconductor production outside of Silicon Valley is more likely to involve high-volume routinized manufacture of standardized integrated circuits and low-technology discrete devices, as shown by table 7.10. Thus, the computed discriminant scores are significantly correlated with the following additional variables (with the sign of the correlation shown in parentheses):
(a) percentage of employees engaged in circuit design (positive),
(b) percentage of output composed of integrated circuits (positive),
(c) percentage of output composed of discrete devices (negative),
(d) age of fabrication equipment (negative),
(e) average feature-size (negative—for feature size is inversely related to the level of technological sophistication of the production process).
Observe that table 7.10 also informs us that Silicon-Valley plants tend to be very specialized in the sense that they typically do little assembly work on-site, and have a propensity to farm out assembly to independent subcontractors. At the same time, table 7.10 indicates once more that Silicon-Valley plants are overwhelmingly tied to local markets. There appears to be little difference between Silicon-Valley producers and non-Silicon-Valley producers in matters such as plant size, production workers as a percentage of all employees, female workers as a percentage of all employees, and the wages of production workers. The signs of the correlation coefficients associated with these variables, however, suggest that Silicon-Valley producers are marginally smaller, have slightly lower ratios of blue-collar to white-collar workers, and pay marginally higher wages than non-Silicon-Valley producers. Once more, the results presented in table 7.10 are satisfactory for the case of all establishments and integrated circuit producers, whereas the results for discrete producers are rather indefinite. Presumably this state of affairs is again a consequence of the fact that the production of low-technology discrete devices in the USA is comparatively independent of the very specialized agglomeration economies of Silicon Valley.

Towards a wider context of analysis
The geography of the on-shore semiconductor industry in the USA is thus marked by a primary twofold pattern of agglomeration and dispersal. The driving locational focus of the industry today is Silicon Valley, with its stock of specialized agglomeration economies. It is in this highly flexible and transactions-intensive environment that much of the leading edge, low-volume, custom, and semicustom flexible productive activity is concentrated. So far, this end of the production spectrum has been relatively resistant to the incursions of Japanese competition, whereas larger merchant producers of

standardized mass-produced devices (memory circuits especially) have exhibited much less resilience. Outside of Silicon Valley, we observe a spatial sequence of less important clusters of establishments, many of them contained within all-purpose electronics production complexes, along with a dispersed locational pattern involving relatively routinized forms of semi-conductor manufacture together with increasing numbers of captive plants.

These intricate locational structures are intertwined with a wider international division of labor in the semiconductor industry. This inter-national division of labor is manifest above all in the spatial/functional separation between onshore wafer fabrication (and other front-end operations) and offshore chip assembly (together with increasing amounts of final test activities). As I have argued elsewhere (see Scott, 1987), the performance of assembly functions offshore in branch plants owned by US semiconductor firms can be interpreted as a search for various location-specific advantages—among them cheap labor—under circumstances where the presence of firm-specific capital of one sort or another inhibits externalization. Such plants are therefore vertically integrated within the firm but geographically separated from its other internal units. They are able to operate effectively at locations distant from these units because it is comparatively easy (despite the firm-specific capital involved) to establish and maintain simple transactional structures consisting for the most part of a single production line extending from the United States to, say, East and Southeast Asia and back again. The locational forces at work in this kind of relationship are the very converse of those that come into play where linkages are multifarious and ever-changing, and they give rise to converse geographical results, namely, dispersal as opposed to agglomeration. This remark provides an alternative perspective on the theoretical arguments marshalled above, and a further confirmation of them.

8

Synthesis

In this book, I have dealt with a series of theoretical issues that seem to me to represent essential underpinnings for any attempt to understand the meaning of the new industrial spaces that are now taking shape throughout the advanced capitalist societies as Fordism gives way to flexible accumulation. I have also dealt in detail with three major case studies, each representing a particular kind of functional and spatial response to the new imperatives of production flexibility. It is evident from the emphasis that I have placed upon these case studies that I attribute much importance to their individual empirical specificities and to the need to acknowledge the integrity of their individual historical trajectories. It is, however, equally important that we pay close attention to the possibility of arriving at some wider theoretical conclusions regarding the overall geographical dynamics of the turn to flexible production organization. I now therefore attempt to draw up a brief and roughly delineated tableau concerning what we evidently know in general—and what remains open for future investigation—about new industrial spaces and the dense growth centers that constitute their inner cores in the emerging regime of flexible accumulation.

The macrogeography of production
The dominant features of any regime of capitalist accumulation are in important ways defined by the technology systems, organizational structure, and labor relations of the principal sectoral ensembles on which the regime is based. The era of Fordist mass production can certainly be sharply identified in terms of these criteria, and they seem just as readily to distinguish the regime of flexible accumulation that is currently gathering momentum in the advanced capitalist societies. In the present account, two particular kinds of ensembles (namely artisanal production and high-technology industry) have been given special attention, though services also constitute (and to an ever-increasing degree) a highly symptomatic set of flexible production sectors. Each of these ensembles represents groups of sectors that typically produce extremely variable outputs in short runs, and that face rapidly changing markets in a climate of resurgent economic competition. They are also given to pronounced social divisions of labor in their organizational structure, leading, as we have seen, to a proliferation of external economies of scale and thence to the formation of agglomerated production complexes.

At the same time, as these ensembles have grown in importance within the advanced capitalist economies, corresponding macrogeographic changes have occurred. In some instances, to be sure, flexible production complexes have simply recolonized sites located in or adjacent to older industrial spaces dating from earlier eras of accumulation. This is the case, for example, with high-technology industrial development in parts of

Central Scotland or South Wales (cf Morgan and Sayer, 1985). As pointed out in chapter 2, this sort of recolonization has usually been accompanied by decisive attempts to squeeze the traditional male working class out of concomitant employment opportunities. To a major degree, however, the ascending ensembles of the new regime have simply forsaken areas that developed on the basis of earlier rounds of accumulation and they have tended to grow at alternative locations where the process of accumulation can be reconstructed with minimal hindrance from residues of previously formed social responses to direct encounters with industrialization. The logic of this latter kind of geographic shift merits some further consideration in the present context, and here I briefly recapitulate the discussion in chapter 2.

In long-established industrial regions, such as the Manufacturing Belt of the United States or the Midlands of England, extended traditions of working-class organization and industrial conflict are common. This phenomenon is expressed in an accumulated historical experience of labor militancy, usually accompanied by high rates of worker unionization and the assertion of established privileges in the workplace. Despite the circumstance that the masses of workers remaining in these regions have tended recently to lower their expectations about their general conditions of employment, they remain, from the point of view of capitalist employers, contaminated by their own past. More directly, the old centers of Fordist industry face the continuing problem of rigidified labor relations and work rules and a consequent narrowing of the margin of managerial manoeuver. This problem is especially serious for production sectors that are experiencing high rates of innovation and where process and product configurations are liable to change at frequent intervals so that job definitions and workers' responsibilities are also susceptible to rapid modification. Enterprises in such sectors will, we may surmise, actively seek out correspondingly flexible organizational and labor-market arrangements. If they are located in older industrial regions they may attempt to secure this objective by a combined strategy of agglomerating together at particular sites and employing a particular kind of labor force in such a way as to exclude, as far as possible, traditional working-class elements. Another way of securing the same exclusionary objective, and one that is almost certainly less problematical (since the historical traditions and geographical structure of a place can never simply be reconstructed over again) is to shift the process of accumulation onto altogether fresh terrain where radically new sorts of sociotechnical formations can be forged with relative ease.

Hence, to a large degree, the new industrial ensembles of the regime of flexible accumulation first emerged onto the scene of modern capitalism with a general aversion to locations too close to the old centers of mass production; and they were, for a time at least, comparatively footloose. A social division of labor had not yet begun to form in any major way within most of the sectors composing these ensembles and they had not yet engendered large specialized local labor markets; as a result, their locational behavior was initially relatively independent of external economies and agglomerative forces. Many producers in these ensembles thus became established at peripheral locations that may well at the outset have appeared to have few potentialities for massive industrialization. Once producers were rooted in those locations, of course, the play of the evolving social division of labor and concomitant local labor-market phenomena rapidly— in some cases at least—started to induce strong developmental effects in the local area. In brief, as a number of new centers of industrial growth began to take shape in some areas, their expanding field of agglomeration economies turned them increasingly into the privileged locational foci of the evolving regime of flexible accumulation.

Those broad areas that have been most susceptible to the formation of new flexible growth centers seem to share a number of environmental qualities (though, conversely, not all areas with these qualities have become the bases of new growth center formation). Three particular types of geographical environment have evidently played an especially important role in the macrogeographical definition of the regime. First, as noted, some traditional craft communities, above all in the Third Italy and to a lesser degree in other parts of Western Europe, have been the sites of a significant industrial revival in the recent past. Second, many small and medium-sized towns in areas previously lacking in significant industrial development have attracted much new manufacturing activity, as exemplified by many booming high-technology industrial centers in the US Sunbelt (such as Austin, Boulder, or Colorado Springs) and in Western Europe (such as Cambridge, Grenoble, or Montpellier). Third, there has been, too, much growth of high-technology industry in suburban areas adjacent to major metropolitan regions. In the United States, these suburban technopoles are heavily concentrated in the Sunbelt (as, for example, in the cases of Orange County or Silicon Valley), though there are exceptions to this observation, as manifest above all by Boston's Route 128. The Scientific City in France is the outstanding Western European example of an expanding suburban technopole.

By way of contrast with these three cases, the service industry along with a number of long-standing inner-city flexible-manufacturing communities (engaged in producing clothing, furniture, jewelry, etc) have retained a comparatively close association with older concentrations of economic activity and human settlement. Even in these instances, however, the primary locational and social bases of productive labor differ notably from those that sustained Fordist mass production. The service industry is to be found mainly in the central business districts and suburban communities of large metropolitan regions where it employs managerial and white-collar fractions of the labor force together with large numbers of female workers in the lowest-paid jobs; and inner-city manufacturing communities focused on flexible production systems are to ever-increasing degrees dependent on a disorganized lumpenproletariat composed largely of immigrant and female workers.

The concrete unfolding of these geographical relationships over the last couple of decades has had as its counterpart a steady deterioration in the economic and political power of the old working class in many formerly prosperous industrial regions. Large numbers of communities have simply been abandoned by industry, resulting in extensive pools of unemployed workers and fiscally crippled municipal governments. In other instances, a recomposition and redisciplining of the traditional working class has been occurring as the regressive labor-market norms and practices currently developing in the new centers of accumulation throughout the world are imported back into the old. Even mass-production industries are now experimenting on a major scale with more flexible forms of organization and labor relations, ranging from robotization and just-in-time delivery systems to workers' quality circles, four-day work weeks, and dramatically simplified systems of job categories. What has been occurring, both in old and in new industrial sectors, is a drastic and highly successful attack on the rigidities and predicaments of production bequeathed by earlier rounds of accumulation. In this process, both the social life and the geographic landscape of modern capitalism are being fundamentally transformed.

The internal logic of territorial production complexes
In many different parts of North America and Western Europe, then, new industrial spaces are coming into being and are growing apace. Each is a unique case. Each seems to have had its own idiosyncratic moment of genesis, and each its particular subsequent history; and each also represents a very specific articulation of local social conditions with the wider coordinates of capitalist development in general. It is always of historical interest to note the empirical circumstances that have attended the beginnings of any given center of industrialization (for example, preexisting craft traditions, spin-offs from isolated plants, the presence of particularly energetic and far-sighted individuals, and the like), though there are also, no doubt, as many possible anecdotes about these matters as there are individual cases. In theoretical terms, the most interesting and important issues would seem to lie elsewhere, and I propose that they are especially to be found in the question of the developmental logic of growth centers as spatially concentrated systems of production characterized by much social division of labor and local labor-market activity. It is worth stressing that this problem cannot be dealt with by a simple description of the micro-geographic origins of any particular center, as, for example, in the slippage that occurs in some of the literature on Silicon Valley, which begins with the observation that the initiation of the semiconductor industry there coincided with the activities of Terman and Shockley and then shifts to the implied conclusion that this information somehow helps us understand the way things are today.

What I have tried to demonstrate in this book is that the new industrial spaces of the regime of flexible accumulation can most effectively be comprehended as *transactions-intensive agglomerations of human labor and social activity* triggered by epochal change and renewal in the broad pattern of capitalist industrialization. Out of this tense force-field of relations there has emerged at particular places in the recent past a powerful and self-reinforcing spiral of growth, sustained by the endogenous creation of external economies of scale. Under specifiable interindustrial linkage conditions, these external economies are transformed into agglomeration benefits by the locational behavior of producers, and are hence finally consumed within localized production complexes. So long as markets for final outputs are expanding, or at least stable, the whole system can continue—in principle—to evolve internally by means of a deepening social division of labor and increasing elaboration of local labor-market structures. In this context, technological innovation, entrepreneurial activity, and genealogical structures of horizontal and vertical firm spin-off become the proximate expressions of the underlying logic and pattern of growth. In particular, a process of territorial reproduction is set in motion in which the production system and the social system come simultaneously to depend upon and yet to sustain one another's existence. Additionally, individual producers in different growth centers develop multiple transactional relations with one another, so that these centers eventually form a mesh of interlocking local economies evolving interdependently through time.

The very forces that drive forward the expansion of industrial growth centers, however, may also on occasions bring about their stagnation and demise. More than anything else, critical ruptures in the historical path of technological and organizational evolution may decisively undercut pre-existing patterns of spatially convergent development and bring about resynthesis and spatial dispersal of production activities. Such a turn of events has occurred repeatedly in the past, and most recently in the regime of Fordist accumulation where the perfection of routinized and deskilled mass-production processes suitable for operation in dispersed branch plants has had a devastating effect on older industrial regions. By the same token, we must leave ourselves open to the speculation that the burgeoning new industrial spaces identified in these pages may one day find their trajectory of growth reversed and their economic life deranged by permanent crisis and decay.

Finale: the sociocultural foundations of new industrial spaces in the regime of flexible accumulation

The new flexible manufacturing complexes that have sprung up at various locations since the end of the Second World War have thus for the most part appeared in geographic areas that have had little or no prior history of industrialization and working-class community development. The areas that have been most intensively colonized by these complexes usually have accommodating sociocultural environments in which resistance to flexibility of production relations and labor-market arrangements, and all it stands for, is at a low level. Hence, in the Third Italy, industrial growth has occurred within traditional communities where class polarization is subdued and where an inherited spirit of small entrepreneurship is strongly developed. Even though many municipalities in the Third Italy are on the left of the political spectrum, they have warmly welcomed artisanal enterprise which is seen as being relatively benign both socially and environmentally. In the Scientific City of the southern Ile de France, much of the working-class population has been communally reconstituted in the two new towns, and for the rest, we find mainly low-density suburban forms of settlement dominated by middle strata. Throughout the area of the Scientific City, access to environmental amenities in the shape of rural and semirural open space is high and, moreover, the area lies immediately adjacent to what will eventually become Europe's Disneyland, with all that that implies for patterns of socialization and social reproduction. In Silicon Valley—and in the Sunbelt at large—there tend to be sharp communal divisions between high-income managerial and technical cadres much imbued with neo-conservative attitudes, and low-income ethnic groups many of them undocumented immigrants (a circumstance that points at once to their political marginality and hence to their particular value as unskilled workers). In spite of important and evident differences between these three examples, they all have one common denominator: forms of social being are in each case more or less consonant with efficient and smoothly ordered production under conditions of organizational and labor-market flexibility. In all three cases, producers have, as it were, been able to discover and exploit those positive human qualities made fortuitously available to them by the circumstances of history and geography. More generally, precisely because such circumstances exist across a wide geographic front, the spatial bases of accumulation are today being radically reconstructed; and, in their turn, these same spatial bases with their varying but accommodating socio-cultural attributes have become a major factor in the accelerating development of the regime of flexible accumulation.

It is no doubt tempting to take these sociocultural attributes at face value, that is, in the terms in which they appear to us on a first cursory empirical examination. In these terms, what we see is something that is often conventionally referred to as a 'high quality of life'. For example, in the case of emerging industrial communities in the Sunbelt two significant indices contribute to this perception. One is the absence of the physical disorder, urban deterioration, and class consciousness typical of older industrial communities. The other is their abundant low-density tract housing, highly privatized forms of family life, a diversity of recreational resources, and a positive business climate (or, in another vocabulary, low local tax rates and pro-growth municipal administrations). Some analysts have claimed that these sorts of qualities are attractive to skilled scientific and technical workers who accordingly throng to places where they are to be found. Employers who depend on these workers presumably then have no option but to follow the locational inclinations of their main labor force, and this supposedly helps to account for industrial development in such places. The problem here is not that many communities in the Sunbelt and elsewhere fail to exhibit qualities of these sorts; on the contrary, those enumerated above constitute a reasonably accurate description, insofar as it goes, of some of their prevailing characteristics. The objection I want to raise is that, by assimilating the visible appearance of these characteristics into a purely ideological notion of the quality of life, we lose sight of their underlying social meaning. We lose sight, in particular, of the circumstance that they are not so much independent variables in a chain of causal relations that begins with the alleged tastes and preferences of scientific and technical workers and ends with the shift of high-technology industry to the Sunbelt, but are contingent conditions incorporated within the regime of accumulation where they actively support the reproduction of social and economic relations. In any given case, rounds of expansion in the local industrial base will bring more and more workers within the ambit of the production system and thence into the socializing sphere of local community life. This phenomenon is not, however, the expression of naked and unmediated volition on the part of workers, but an effect of the expansionary logic of the whole system.

These elements of the social milieu of industrial centers find their central point of concentration in what we might call a politics of place, namely, a continually evolving system of localized collective human responses to the dynamics of daily work and life in the community (cf Scott and Storper, 1987). In the old centers of Fordist mass production, the politics of place has developed over several decades and through innumerable vicissitudes to the point where producers have in many cases simply abandoned them. In the new centers of flexible production springing forth on the contemporary landscape of capitalism, a more complaisant system of relationships between the workplace and the community appears to be currently detectable, and many of these centers seem poised on the threshold of a long, if uneasy, industrial peace.

History, nonetheless, is in the making even here. One of the most intriguing questions about these centers is how their politics of place will change with the passage of time. Will they continue to remain socially and industrially in a state of relative calm? Or will a newly militant working class emerge, self-aware and ready to confront again the hegemony of capitalist business and labor relations? The unfolding historical geography of what are today the new industrial spaces of capitalism will most certainly provide a fertile terrain for future observation and research.

References

Aglietta M, 1979 *A Theory of Capitalist Regulation: The US Experience* (New Left Books, London)

Agostinelli S, Russi M, Salmoni V, 1983, "L'industrializzazione diffusa nelle Marche: aspetti urbanistici", in *Industrializzazione senza Fratture* Eds G Fuà, C Zacchia (Il Mulino, Bologna) pp 67–101

Alchian A A, Demsetz H, 1972, "Production, information costs, and economic organization" *American Economic Review* **62** 777–795

Annuaire des Biotechnologies et des Bioindustries, 1987, Association pour le Développement de la Bio-Industrie (Biofutur, Paris)

Bagnasco A, 1977 *Tre Italie: La Problematica Territoriale dello Sviluppo Italiano* (Il Mulino, Bologna)

Bakis H, 1977 *IBM: Une Multinationale Régionale* (Presses Universitaires de Grenoble, Grenoble)

Balestri A, 1982, "Industrial organization in the manufacture of fashion goods: the textile district of Prato (1950–1980)", unpublished MPhil thesis, Department of Economics, University of Lancaster, Lancaster

Bastié J, 1964 *La Croissance de la Banlieue Parisienne* (Presses Universitaires de France, Paris)

Becattini G, 1979, "Dal settore industriale al distretto industriale. Alcune considerazioni sull'unità di indagine dell'economia industriale" *Rivista di Economia e Politica Industriale* number 2, 7–21

Becattini G, 1986, "Buying offices e diffusione sul territorio: due aspetti dello sviluppo delle piccole e medie imprese in Toscana", in *Papers de Seminari* number 25/26, Centre d'Estudis de Planificación, pp 23–32

Becattini G, 1987, "L'unità d'indagine", in *Mercato e Forze Locali: Il Distretto Industriale* Ed. G Becattini (Il Mulino, Bologna) pp 35–48

Becattini G, Bellandi M, Faloni A, 1983, "L'industrializzazione diffusa in Toscana: aspetti economici", in *Industrializzazione senza Fratture* Eds G Fuà, C Zacchia (Il Mulino, Bologna) pp 47–66

Bellandi M, 1986, "The Marshallian Industrial District" Studie Discussioni number 42, Dipartimento di Scienze Economiche, Università degli Studi di Firenze

Bellandi M, 1987, "La formulazione originaria", in *Mercato e Forze Locali: Il Distretto Industriale* Ed. G Becattini (Il Mulino, Bologna) pp 49–67

Bernstein A, DeGrasse B, Grossman R, Paine C, Siegel L, 1977 *Silicon Valley: Paradise or Paradox? The Impact of High Technology Industry on Santa Clara County* Pacific Studies Center, Mountain View, CA

Bluestone B, Harrison B, 1982 *The Deindustrialization of America* (Basic Books, New York)

Böhm-Bawerk E von, 1891 *The Positive Theory of Capital* (G E Stechert, New York)

Borts G H, Stein J L, 1964 *Economic Growth in a Free Market* (Columbia University Press, New York)

Boyer R, 1986 *La Théorie de la Régulation: Une Analyse Critique* (Editions la Découverte, Paris)

Braun E, MacDonald S, 1982 *Revolution in Miniature* (Cambridge University Press, Cambridge)

Brocard M, 1981, "Aménagement du territoire et développement régional: le cas de la recherche scientifique" *L'Espace Géographique* **7** 61–73

Brusco S, 1982, "The Emilian model: productive decentralisation and social integration" *Cambridge Journal of Economics* **6** 167–184

Brusco S, 1983, "Flessibilità e solidità del sistema: l'esperienza emiliana'", in *Industrializzazione senza Fratture* Eds G Fuà, C Zacchia (Il Mulino, Bologna) pp 103–124

Brusco S, 1986, "Small firms and industrial districts: the experience of Italy", in *New Firms and Regional Development in Europe* Eds D Keeble, E Wever (Croom Helm, Beckenham, Kent) pp 184–202

Business Directories Inc., 1985 *Rich's Business Guide to Santa Clara County's Silicon Valley* (Business Directories Inc., Los Altos, CA)

Castells M, 1975 *Sociologie de l'Espace Industriel* (Editions Anthropos, Paris)

Censimento Generale dell'Industria del Commercio, del Servizi et dell'Artigianato (various years), Instituto Centrale di Statistica, Rome

Census of Manufactures (various years), US Department of Commerce, Bureau of the Census (US Government Printing Office, Washington, DC)

Census of Population and Housing, 1980, US Department of Commerce, Bureau of the Census (US Government Printing Office, Washington, DC)

Cenzatti M, 1986, "Industrial restructuring in Italy: a literature review, 1970–1985", unpublished paper, School of Architecture and Urban Planning, University of California, Los Angeles, CA

Clark G L, 1986, "The crisis of the Midwest auto industry", in *Production, Work, Territory: The Geographical Anatomy of Industrial Capitalism* Eds A J Scott, M Storper (Allen and Unwin, Winchester, MA) pp 127–148

Coase R H, 1937, "The nature of the firm" *Economica* 4 386–405

Cooke P, 1985, "Regional innovation policy: problems and strategies in Britain and France" *Environment and Planning C: Government and Policy* 3 253–267

Cooke P, 1987, "Piccolo è bello" *The Geographical Magazine* October issue, 498–502

County Business Patterns (various years), US Department of Commerce, Bureau of the Census (US Government Printing Office, Washington, DC)

CSAU, 1985 *Cité Scientifique: Perception et Propositions d'Actions* Cycle Supérieur d'Aménagement et d'Urbanisme, Institut d'Etudes Politiques, Paris

CSAU, 1986 *Pour un Technopôle en Ile de France Sud: Données et Enjeux* Cycle Supérieur d'Aménagement et d'Urbanisme, Institut d'Etudes Politiques, Paris

Danon G, 1986 *Pour une Politique Régionale de la Recherche et la Technologie en Ile-de-France* Ministère de la Recherche et de la Technologie, Délégation Régionale à la Recherche et à la Technologie de l'Ile de France Sud, Paris

Davoine G, Rouault D, Rousset-Deschamps M, 1985 *Recherche et Industrie en Ile de France Sud: Eléments d'Identification d'une Cité Scientifique* Unité d'Enseignement et de Recherche Lettres Géographie, Institut d'Urbanisme de Paris, Université de Paris XII, Val de Marne

Decoster E, Tabariés M, 1986, "L'innovation dans un pôle scientifique et technologique: le cas de la Cité Scientifique Ile de France Sud", in *Milieux Innovateurs en Europe* Ed. P Aydalot, Groupe de Recherche Européen sur les Milieux Innovateurs, Paris, pp 79–100

Del Monte A, Giannola A, 1986, "Relevance and nature of small and medium-sized firms in Southern Italy", in *New Firms and Regional Development in Europe* Eds D Keeble, E Wever (Croom Helm, Beckenham, Kent) pp 275–298

Dorfman N S, 1983, "Route 128: the development of a regional high technology economy" *Research Policy* 12 299–316

Dosi G, 1984 *Technical Change and Industrial Transformation* (Macmillan, London)

Dunford M, 1988 *Capital, the State, and Regional Development* (Pion, London)

Employment Hours and Earnings, States and Areas Bulletins 1370-17 and 1370-19 (various years), US Department of Labour (US Government Printing Office, Washington, DC)

FIEE, 1985 *Rapport Annuel* Fédération des Industries Electriques et Electroniques, Paris

Fiorentini R, 1983, "Economia periferica ed area tipica", in *L'Apertura Internazionale di un'Economia Periferica* Ed. E Benedetti (Cleup Editore, Padova) pp 84–99

Freeman C, Clark J, Soete L, 1982 *Unemployment and Technical Innovation: A Study of Long Waves and Economic Development* (Greenwood Press, Westport, CT)

Fröbel F, Heinrichs J, Kreye O, 1980 *The New International Division of Labour* (Cambridge University Press, Cambridge)

Fuà G, 1983, "Rural industrialization in later developed countries: The case of northeast and central Italy" *Banca Nazionale del Lavoro Quarterly Review* December issue, 351–377

Ganne B, 1983 *Gens du Cuir, Gens du Papier* (Editions du Centre National de la Recherche Scientifique, Paris)

Garofoli G, 1981, "Lo sviluppo delle 'aree periferiche' nell'economia italiana degli anni settanta" *L'Industria* number 3, 391–404

Garofoli G, 1983a *Industrializzazione Diffusa in Lombardia* (Franco Angeli, Milan)

Garofoli G, 1983b, "Sviluppo regionale e ristrutturazione industriale: il modello italiano degli anni '70" *Rassegna Economica* 47 1263–1295

GARP, 1985 *Effectif des Salariés 31 décembre 1984, II—Les Départements de la Région d'Ile de France* Groupement des ASSEDIC de la Région Parisienne, Paris

Glasmeier A, 1985 *Spatial Differentiation of High Technology Industries: Implications for Planning* PhD dissertation, Department of City and Regional Planning, University of California, Berkeley, CA

Green S, 1983, "Silicon Valley's women workers: a theoretical analysis of sex segregation in the electronics industry labor market", in *Women, Men, and the International Division of Labor* Eds J Nash, M P Fernandez-Kelly (State University of New York Press, Albany, NY) pp 273–331

Guieysse J-A, 1983 *La Recherche Scientifique et Technique dans l'Industrie: le Cas de la Région Parisienne* unpublished doctoral dissertation (2 volumes), Laboratoire de l'Analyse de l'Espace, University of Paris I, Paris

Hall P G, 1962, "The East London footwear industry: an industrial quarter in decline" *East London Papers* 5 3–21

Hirschman A, 1958 *The Strategy of Economic Development* (Yale University Press, New Haven, CT)

Hoover E M, Vernon R, 1959 *Anatomy of a Metropolis* (Harvard University Press, Cambridge, MA)

Husson J-L, 1979 *Evolution de l'Industrie en Région d'Ile-de-France (1962–1976)* Institut d'Aménagement et d'Urbanisme de la Région d'Ile-de-France, Paris

IAURIF, 1984 *La Filière Electronique en Ile-de-France* Institut d'Aménagement et d'Urbanisme de la Région d'Ile-de-France, Paris

Jayet H, 1983, "Chômer plus souvent en région urbaine, plus longtemps en région rurale" *Economie et Statistique* 153 47–57

Kaldor N, 1970, "The case for regional policies" *Scottish Journal of Political Economy* 17 337–348

King R, 1985 *The Industrial Geography of Italy* (Croom Helm, Beckenham, Kent)

Kompass Régional Ile de France, 1987 1987 (Société Nouvelle d'Editions pour l'Industrie, Paris)

Lipietz A, 1986, "New tendencies in the international division of labor: regimes of accumulation and modes of regulation", in *Production, Work, Territory: The Geographical Anatomy of Industrial Capitalism* Eds A J Scott, M Storper (Allen and Unwin, Winchester, MA) pp 16 40

Mandel E, 1980 *Long Waves of Capitalist Development* (Cambridge University Press, Cambridge)

Marshall A, 1920 *Principles of Economics* (Macmillan, London)

Marshall A, 1932 *Industry and Trade* 3rd edition (Macmillan, London)

Massey D, Meegan R, 1982 *The Anatomy of Job Loss* (Methuen, Andover, Hants)

Mezzino A, 1985, "Sviluppo settoriale e organizzazione territoriale di un'area di piccola impresa: il caso del distretto di Pesaro", in *Piccola Città e Piccola Impresa* Ed. R Innocenti (Franco Angeli, Milan) pp 269–299

Michelsons A, 1985, "La problematica dell'industrializzazione diffusa nelle scienze sociali italiane", in *Piccola Città e Piccola Impresa* Ed. R Innocenti (Franco Angeli, Milan) pp 73–98

Morgan K, Sayer A, 1985, "A modern industry in a mature region: the restructuring of labour-management relations" *International Journal of Urban and Regional Research* **9** 383–404

Mossello M T, 1987, "Economie di agglomerazione e sviluppo economico", in *Mercato e Forze Locali: Il Distretto Industriale* Ed. G Becattini (Il Mulino, Bologna) pp 93–116

Murray R, 1985, "Benetton Britain: the new economic order" *Marxism Today* **11** 28–32

Myrdal G, 1957 *Economic Theory and Underdeveloped Regions* (Harper and Row, New York)

Noë P, 1982 *Cité Scientifique, Ile-de-France Sud* Rapport au Ministre de l'Industrie et de la Recherche, Palais du Luxembourg, Paris

OECD, 1986 *La Politique d'Innovation en France* Organisation for Economic Cooperation and Development, Paris (copublished by Economica, Paris)

Oi W Y, 1962, "Labor as a quasi-fixed factor" *Journal of Political Economy* **73** 538–555

Peyrache V, 1984 *La Localisation des Etablissements à Haute Technologie en Région Ile-en-France* Mémoire pour le Diplôme d'Etudes Approfondies d'Espace et Environnement, Université de Paris I, Paris

Phelps E S (Ed.), 1973 *The Microeconomic Foundations of Employment and Inflation Theory* (W W Norton, New York)

Piore M J, Sabel C F, 1983, "Italian small business development: lessons for U.S. industrial policy", in *American Industry in International Competition: Government Policies and Corporate Strategies* Eds J Zysman, L Tyson (Cornell University Press, Ithaca, NY) pp 391–421

Piore M J, Sabel C F, 1984 *The Second Industrial Divide* (Basic Books, New York)

Raveyre M F, Saglio J, 1984, "Les systèmes industriels localisés: éléments pour une analyse sociologique des ensembles de P.M.E. industriels" *Sociologie du Travail* **2** 157–176

Recensement Général de la Population de 1982, 1982 Institut National de la Statistique et des Etudes Economiques, Paris

Richardson G B, 1972, "The organization of industry" *Economic Journal* **83** 883–896

Roberts E B, Wainer H A, 1968, "New enterprises along Route 128" *Science Journal* **2** 79–83

Rogers E, Larson J, 1984 *Silicon Valley Fever* (Basic Books, New York)

Russo M, 1985, "Technical change and the industrial district: the role of interfirm relations in the growth and transformation of ceramic tile production in Italy" *Research policy* **14** 329–343

Savy M, 1986, "Les territoires de l'innovation. Technopôles et aménagement: l'expérience française" *Revue d'Economie Régionale et Urbaine* number 1, 41–60

Saxenian A, 1983, "The urban contradictions of Silicon Valley" *International Journal of Urban and Regional Research* **17** 237–261

Schumpeter J A, 1950 *Capitalism, Socialism and Democracy* (Harper and Row, New York)

Scott A J, 1981, "The spatial structure of metropolitan labor markets and the theory of intra-urban plant location" *Urban Geography* **2** 1–30

Scott A J, 1983, "Industrial organization and the logic of intra-metropolitan location II: a case study of the printed circuits industry in the Greater Los Angeles region" *Economic Geography* **59** 343–367

Scott A J, 1984, "Territorial reproduction and transformation in a local labor market: the animated film workers of Los Angeles" *Environment and Planning D: Society and Space* **2** 277–307

Scott A J, 1987, "The semiconductor industry in South-East Asia: organization, location and the international division of labour" *Regional Studies* **21** 143–160

Scott A J, 1988 *Metropolis: From the Division of Labor to Urban Form* (University of California Press, Berkeley, CA)

Scott A J, Storper M, 1987, "High technology industry and regional development: a theoretical critique and reconstruction" *International Social Science Journal* number 112, 215–232

Sirmans C F, 1977, "City size and unemployment: some new estimates" *Urban Studies* **14** 91–101

Smith A, 1776, 1970 edition *The Wealth of Nations* (Penguin Books, Harmondsworth, Middx)

Solinas G, 1982, "Labour market segmentation and worker's careers: the case of the Italian knitwear industry" *Cambridge Journal of Economics* **6** 331–352

Sraffa P, 1960 *Production of Commodities by Means of Commodities* (Cambridge University Press, Cambridge)

Stigler G J, 1951, "The division of labor is limited by the extent of the market" *Journal of Political Economy* **59** 185–193

Stigler G J, 1962, "Information in the labor market" *Journal of Political Economy* **70** 94–105

Stoffaës C, 1978 *La Grande Menace Industrielle* (Calmann-Lévy, Paris)

Storper M, Christopherson S, 1987, "Flexible specialization and regional industrial agglomeration: the case of the U.S. motion picture industry" *Annals of the Association of American Geographers* **77** 104–117

Taylor M J, Thrift N J, 1982, "Industrial linkages and the segmented economy: 1. Some theoretical proposals" *Environment and Planning A* **14** 1601–1613

Vernon R, 1960 *Metropolis 1985* (Harvard University Press, Cambridge, MA)

Vipond J, 1974, "City size and unemployment" *Urban Studies* **11** 39–46

Williamson O E, 1975 *Markets and Hierarchies: Analysis and Antitrust Implications* (Free Press, New York)

Williamson O E, 1985 *The Economic Institutions of Capitalism* (Free Press, New York)

Young A, 1928, "Increasing returns and economic progress" *Economic Journal* **38** 527–542

Zacchia C, 1984, "Rural industrialization in Italy" *Journal of World Trade Law* **18** 110–124

Index